IMMORTALS
FENYX RISING
A Traveler's Guide to the Golden Isle

IMMORTALS
FENYX RISING

A Traveler's Guide to the Golden Isle

By Zeus
As told to Rick Barba

DARK HORSE BOOKS

president and publisher
MIKE RICHARDSON

editor
IAN TUCKER

associate editor
BRETT ISRAEL

designer
SKYLER WEISSENFLUH

digital art technician
ANN GRAY

IMMORTALS FENYX RISING: A TRAVELER'S GUIDE TO THE GOLDEN ISLE

Published by Dark Horse Books
A division of Dark Horse Comics LLC
10956 SE Main Street
Milwaukie, OR 97222

DarkHorse.com

Ebook ISBN 978-1-50672-056-2
Hardcover ISBN 978-1-50672-048-7

First edition: September 2022

1 3 5 7 9 10 8 6 4 2
Printed in China

MIX
Paper from
responsible sources
FSC® C109093

CONTENTS

Author's Preface

I have many people to thank for their generous help and support during the arduous process of writing this book.

First off, thanks to my folks, Kronos and Rhea, without whom I might have grown up happy and well adjusted. Dad, special thanks for devouring my other siblings whole. Watching Mother force you to disgorge them was easily the most formative moment of my career.

Okay, I'm kidding. Nobody helped me write this book. I don't need "support." I'm Zeus, for god's sake.

However, I will express a certain appreciation to someone who kept me amused while I "labored" (ha ha) on this book. (I basically wrote it in my sleep.) My dear Prometheus, viewing your daily torment really sharpened my aesthetic sensibilities, and helped keep me grounded. For that, I owe you. Also, I'll never serve liver at a dinner party, I can tell you that.

Beyond this, all of the accolades belong to me: Zeus, head god. Some call me Father of the Gods, and for good reason. You know the reason. Don't make me spell it out for you. Look, my personal symbol is the thunderbolt. *Boom!* Got it?

Anyway, good readers, I invite you to think of this book as your indispensable travel guide to the ancient island of Chryse because, well, that's what it is—an indispensable travel guide to the ancient island of Chryse. But that's not *all* it is. By design, it also doubles as a pocket guide to the lore of the Golden Isle. Chryse is a repository of many, many tales, great and small.

Some may call them legends . . . myths, even. I call them snapshots of my dysfunctional family.

Folks, welcome to my island!

◇ ◇ ◇

Here's a nice bird's-eye view of Chryse. (One could even call it an Ikaros-eye view, but that would be cruel. Funny, but cruel.)

Welcome to the Golden Isle!

Ladies and gents, there's no place quite like Chryse, the vacation island of the gods—not even Mount Olympos itself, to tell you the truth.

Not that Chryse is *better* than Olympos, not even close—I mean, nothing is quite as sacred as the place where gods officially live. But let's be honest, "sacred" is often (or possibly always) boring. Pretentious. The Mount Olympos crowd can be a bit holier than thou, to tell you the truth.

But the Golden Isle is definitely more *fun*. Interesting fauna, really crazy monsters. So much to do! And it's a *dazzling* place —lush valleys, crystal streams, mighty temples, and a majestic mountaintop that puts other mountaintops to shame. Six stunning topographical regions, each unique, each associated with one of the gods. (Mine is best, of course, but the others are . . . not bad.)

Yes, Chryse is a wonderland! It's an island of pristine perfection.

But it's also a really *big* island. Tourists like you will need guidance. So, this traveler's handbook provides you with a detailed map of each region and a comprehensive overview of its topography and vegetation—you know, trees and whatnot. You also get an architectural tour of the most spectacular temples, towers, and statuary this side of Knossos.

Another thing: this *vade mecum*—that's Latin, look it up, I suspect the Romans have a future in these parts—

also directs you to many spots linked to our divine history. Chryse is famous for its intricate, carefully constructed puzzles that, when solved, unlock tales of godly wonder or woe. We gods have been involved in a *lot* of mad stuff. Hey, let's be honest, mental health is not an Olympian strong suit.

So, you really get your money's worth here, is what I'm saying. Would I lie to you? I'm Zeus, right? Take it to the bank.

Oh, one other thing, just a little side note: you may have heard stories of a clash pitting us Olympian gods against a clan of goons called the Titans. Their witless leader, Kronos, my deadbeat dad, was a real sadist. After I knocked him senseless with a few of my best thunderbolts (tossed behind my back, no less), I cast him down into Tartaros. Then my lovely grandmama Gaia sent the worst monster of them all, her son Typhon, a huge horn-headed idiot. He nearly had me beat (he stole my leg muscles, which was like the worst workout ever), but I cast him down into Tartaros too. Then I slammed a mountain on top to seal him into his chamber—the very mountain you see in the center of Chryse today! Isn't that awesome? Now poor, ugly Typhon lumbers around down there, whimpering like a baby goat.

What I'm saying is, if you're trekking around the mountain and hear something that sounds like a sad, angry monster, just ignore it.

Island Origins

Yes, just like the greatest of salad dressings, Chryse is the island of a thousand tales.

But let's start with the one about how this place came to be—the foundational tale, as it were. I'm talking about the legend of Daidalos, the guy who built this island. It includes his dimwit son Ikaros.

Interesting guy, Daidalos. Never met his kid, though.

Here's the inside scoop: this whole island was designed as an elaborate bribe to the gods! Hey, there's not a god I know who wouldn't take a good bribe, including yours truly. And as bribes go, Chryse is one of the best ever. Daidalos was no slouch when it comes to architecture or shady inducement, that's for sure. The Hall of the Gods alone is worth the price of admission.

But let's go back to the beginning, shall we? It all started with a pair of wealthy kings and a so-called "genius" inventor.

◇ ◇ ◇

⋅} *Minos, the Minotaur, and the Flight of Ikaros* {⋅

Back in the day, King Minos of Crete had a beautiful kingdom with a little problem.

A ravenous monster called the Minotaur—half man, half bull—was terrorizing his lands, feasting on human flesh, and putting a big crimp in the holiday shopping season. After consulting the Oracle at Delphi, the king called upon the brilliant architect Daidalos to build a prison beneath the royal palace at Knossos for the creature. Called the Labyrinth, it was designed as an inescapable maze. Daidalos delivered, and King Minos lured the Minotaur into the dark dungeon.

Unfortunately for Daidalos, Minos was also a paranoid lunatic. Since only Daidalos knew the Labyrinth's layout, the king decided to lock him in a tall tower at Knossos, along with his son, Ikaros. The only way to escape the tower was to fly—something that humans don't do, typically. But Daidalos was a genius, right? He crafted two sets of wings, one for himself and

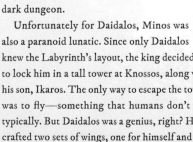

one for Ikaros. Each wing was a wooden frame covered in feathers held in place by wax.

(That's right: wax. The "genius" came up with wax as a feather adherent. I try to remember this every time I'm depressed and need a good laugh.)

Wax, of course, melts when it gets warm. So, as Daidalos practiced flying with Ikaros, he drilled this fact into his son's head, over and over: *Don't fly too high. The sun is hot. Wax melts. Are you listening, boy? Please put down that game and pay attention, will you?*

The big day came. Father and son donned their wings and jumped out of the tower window. The wings worked perfectly! The duo swooped and flapped like strange birds, gliding off the island of Crete and over the Aegean Sea, bearing north to . . . I don't know, wherever their home was. Not sure, really. Don't care. The point is, Daidalos and Ikaros escaped the clutches of the crazy King Minos! But of course, Ikaros—the kid who never paid attention, who played games all day in his room—was so enthralled by the power of effortless flight that he soared straight up toward the sun. His wing wax melted and he plunged like a hundred-pound sack of bones and viscera right into the ocean.

(You might wonder why Ikaros's wings *melted* when in fact the higher you climb into the atmosphere, the colder it actually gets, not hotter. I asked the Muse of Science and Astronomy, Urania, how wax could melt at high altitude instead of, say, freeze, and she told me it has something to do with solar convection or whatever and would I please leave her alone when she's bathing.)

Daidalos was devastated! He dearly loved his stupid son, and blamed himself for the disaster—rightly so, obviously. I mean, the waxy wing thing was *totally* on him. Wracked by guilt and despair, Daidalos banked his own wings westward and flew many, many miles . . . all the way to Sicily!

◇ ◆ ◇

Daidalos: The Sicilian Years

In Sicily, Daidalos found a protector in the powerful King Kokalos, ruler of a kingdom on the island's southwest coast called Kamikos. The bereaved inventor took up residence in the royal palace and mourned the loss of his son. Every day got worse. To help ease his anguish, Daidalos built a temple to Apollo, where he offered his wings as a sacrifice. Yeah, I'm sure Apollo was thrilled.

I don't know where those wings ended up, but I'm sure we'll never see them again.

As he sulked around Kokalos's royal court, Daidalos began to formulate a desperate plan. Ikaros was dead and gone, cast into the Underworld, lost forever . . . or was he? Didn't the Olympian gods have power over Hades and Tartaros? Surely the immensely powerful and wise and super-handsome Zeus could help Daidalos resurrect his son? (I'm just spitballing his thought process here, but it certainly makes sense.)

Meanwhile, back on Crete, things were heating up. King Minos was livid, and he started hunting down his escaped architect. After tracking Daidalos to Sicily, Minos learned he was holed up in the court of King Kokalos. Minos threatened to wreak havoc on Sicilian lands if Daidalos didn't surrender! Being a king himself, Kokalos knew just how to mollify a lunatic—he agreed to hand over Daidalos but first offered Minos a lovely spa day in the Kamikos royal baths.

Who could turn down such an offer? (Not me.) Steam, manicure, massage. Everything seemed destined for a . . . happy ending.

But while Minos was bathing, Daidalos doused him with a cistern of boiling water then chopped him up into twitching gobbets of meat. And I guess the lesson here is: don't mess with a distraught architect?

After that, of course, Daidalos had to skip town, to escape retaliation from Crete. But the exigency of his exit coincided perfectly with the idea blooming inside his feverish, grief-addled brain: *Maybe the gods can help me!* And so Daidalos asked King Kokalos for a few minor favors—a fleet, some engineers, a huge crew of workmen, a few thousand metric tons of building materials, including a big load of precious metals. And apparently Kokalos was like, Sure, no problem.

Setting sail, Daidalos began searching for an uninhabited island to match his vision—someplace with rich variation in topography, a great peak reaching through the clouds, and preferably no homeowner's association or zoning issues. He wanted a place exploding with natural beauty that could complement a wide range of architectural styles.

He found exactly what he was looking for in Chryse.

◇ ◆ ◇

Remember back when I said the Golden Isle was basically a god-sized bribe? Well, here's how it went down.

Once he discovered Chryse, Daidalos got right to work. As the master builder directed multiple construction and landscaping projects across the island, he found himself haunted by his son's death and his gruesome murder of King Minos. His torment twisted itself into some of the architecture—some of the sightlines are kind of ghoulish—but it also drove him to craft something of truly Olympian quality.

Meanwhile, back in Sicily, King Kokalos was having nightmares. The gods were visiting him in his dreams—something we love to do, ha ha—howling and calling the Chryse project an act of hubris to be met with divine retribution. (Hades directed, Dionysos catered, we really had a lot of fun with this.) Shaken, Kokalos set sail for Chryse to stop Daidalos before he provoked punishment.

When the king arrived, he found a spectacular island, finished and perfect. But he couldn't find its builder anywhere. Daidalos had heard the angry king was coming and went into hiding. But he wanted Kokalos to understand his purposes, so he created a series of puzzles that would explain the project origins and lead the king to his workshop.

King Kokalos eventually got there, and . . . well, so did the gods. One of them, anyway. I won't say who. He's big, though. Very major god.

With great pride, Daidalos called on the gods to explore the opulent paradise he had crafted for their exclusive pleasure. A quick group tour confirmed that Chryse was indeed the most beautiful place ever made. Daidalos offered it as a gift to us, asking only that we help him get Ikaros back.

We gods laughed heartily, got drunk, rejected the deal, turned both Daidalos and Kokalos into petrified deer . . . and, yeah, we kept the island anyway.

What can I say? That's how gods roll.

◇ ◈ ◇

⸖ Beneath the Mountain ⸖

Oh, one last thing: that guy under the mountain.

It's just kind of an amusing side note: the island that Daidalos chose for his vanity project, Chryse, just happens to sit atop the eternal prison of the foolish monster who tried to avenge the death of the Titans by taking out us gods. What a loser! After I smote Typhon good, I locked him in a chamber of Tartaros far beneath the center mountain on the Golden Isle. He's been there a *loooooong* time.

Pretty ironic, eh? I love defeating foes, but my favorite part is rubbing it in afterward. So, romping across a godly playground right above Typhon's head for a few eons—you know, it just doesn't get any more satisfying than that.

Sure, he's the ultimate Titan. But it's a big mountain. What could go wrong?

◇ ◈ ◇

Gods and Lesser Beings: A Roster

I'm sometimes shocked at how mortals can be so ignorant of the lives of their gods and heroes. Sure, it's fun to stare at the sky and say, "Hey, is that an eagle?" then watch Prometheus freak out. But it's even more fun if you know the sordid backstory. These days, kids can't even tell the difference between Eros and Eris. What are they teaching in school down there?

Unfortunately, this kind of ignorance is a serious impediment when visiting the Golden Isle. It's hard to get the full immersive experience if you don't know what Daidalos was thinking when he designed some of his myth-based interactive features. Basic god knowledge helps a lot.

So, to help out the Chryse Tourism Board, I've put together a quick compendium of gods and lesser creatures —all the ones represented on this island, anyway.

It's a simple reference tool, alphabetized so even mortals can figure it out. The roll call includes most of the Olympian order, plus various Greek and Trojan heroes. Trust me, almost everybody who's anybody is listed. I even added prominent monsters and chthonic beasts. I did it all from memory, which was easy. I've either slept with or killed most of them.

One last note: Don't be shocked by anything you read. Gods have issues, okay? Some of us have very large appetites. And I'm not just talking lust. We actually eat almost anything—entire boars, large rocks, our wives, our kids. But yeah, lust is a problem too. It's an organizing principle up here. We bang swans, for god's sake.

◇ ◇ ◇

I tried to start off with a family tree—you know, a flow chart of lineage. But god relations are complicated. Lots of "crossover." (That's code for incest and bestiality.) After a while it began to look like a Jackson Pollock fractal cross-drip, so I shelved that project and decided a simple alphabetical list is good enough.

Let's get started, shall we?

Achilles | *Greek Hero of Heroes*

Achilles was the greatest of Greek warriors, hands down. Son of Thetis (god) and Peleus (mortal), he showed more courage, skill, and character than any twelve Argonauts you can toss in a cage. Without him, the Trojan War might have turned out a lot differently for Greece.

Adonis | *Mortal Pretty Boy*

His mom was a myrrh tree, so the nursery situation was weird to say the least. Fortunately, Aphrodite found the infant Adonis in the woods and handed him over to Persephone, queen of the Underworld, for raising. But then tree-boy grew into an astonishing stud, so the two goddesses started fighting over him. Eventually, the problem was solved when Adonis was gored to death by a boar that totally just came out of nowhere, just some random boar. Who could have stopped it? Not me, certainly. Tough luck for the kid. Aphrodite was devastated, and started the Festival of Adonia in his honor—a great party, if you like cabbage and sobbing women.

Aeetes | *Mortal King of Kolkhis*

When Jason and his Argonaut crew arrived in Kolkhis to "acquire" (steal) the Golden Fleece from King Aeetes, he set out tasks for Jason to perform before he'd relinquish the prize. One was to yoke the fire-breathing Kolkhis Bulls—bronze monstrosities crafted by Hephaistos— then use them to plow a field and sow it with dragons' teeth. Sure, no problem! Jason got critical aid from Aeetes's daughter, Medea.

Aiolos | *God of Wind*

This guy's a real blowhard, for sure. He keeps his winds in various jars, for some demented reason. I try not to micromanage my people, but I may need to talk to him about this storage method.

Ajax the Greater | *Mortal Hero*

This Locrian general was a solid soldier. Unfortunately, he's best known as the knucklehead who burst into Athena's temple during the sack of Troy and violated Kassandra, a priestess.

Alektryon the Rooster | *Most Famous Chicken*

Bane of the hung over, this annoying bird shrieks at sunrise every day. Originally a young soldier serving under Ares, Alektryon was posted on guard duty one night outside the room where our randy God of War was engaged in a sweaty tête-à-tête with Aphrodite—yes, his brother's wife. Unfortunately, the poor kid fell asleep. At sunrise, Hephaistos's best buddy Helios walked right past the snoozing guard, found the lovers, and reported the tryst to his friend. As Hephaistos raised hell, an angry Ares turned Alektryon into a rooster who never, ever forgets to announce the rising sun every day, loudly. The upside is he meets a lot of chicks who worship him.

Alkinous | *Mortal King of the Phaikians*

This generous fellow is known for his hospitality to the shipwrecked Odysseus. He owned a sweet palace guarded by fearsome mechanical watchdogs, gifts from Hephaistos.

Andromeda | *Princess Monster Bait*

This poor kid had a bigmouthed mom, Queen Cassiopeia of Aethiopia. (Hey, that rhymes.) Andromeda was gorgeous, so the queen hubristically bragged that her daughter was hotter than even the Nereids, the daughters of Poseidon. This angered my salty brother, so he sent a sea monster named Cetus to terrorize the Aethiopian coast. The only way to appease Poseidon was to feed Andromeda to the monster, so her wonderful mom chained her to a seaside rock. Fortunately, the hero Perseus saved the lovely girl.

Aphrodite | *Goddess of Love and Beauty*

If Aphrodite was mortal, you might call her aggressive. But she's a god, so it's like, yeah, she's super friendly. What a beauty she is! The girl does things with cosmetics that you just wouldn't think possible. I married her off to my son Hephaistos, the blacksmith—I'm thinking stability, good job, steady income. But prostitutes don't worship Aphy as their patron god for her skill in the kitchen. She can't resist bright, shiny objects . . . like Helios, for example. Or Ares. That's right, Heph's own brother!

Apollo | *God of Light, Harmony, Truth, Prophecy, Knowledge, Moderation, Archery, Healing, Poetry, Music, and Eggplant Moussaka*

If ever I were to pass on somehow, my choice of heir would be a tossup between Apollo and Athena. I mean, I'm immortal, so succession is not on the table, ever. But I gotta say, the kid's a baller, just like his twin sister Artemis. Apollo was special from the get-go— quintessence of godly perfection, sees the future, badass archer, the whole package. A little snooty, but that's forgivable when you're archetypal as hell. Oddly, even though he has statues and temples and oracles on Chryse, he just doesn't visit the island anymore. Not sure why. I know he hangs out with the Muses a lot—I think they talked him into directing their godawful summer musicals. It might also have something to do with that flirty Naiad Nymph, Daphne. He's nuts about her.

Arachne | *Leggy Mortal Spinner*

This girl could really spin up some mean cloth. Arachne was easily the best weaver in the business, even better than Athena. Unfortunately, she let everybody know it, and even challenged my wise but sometimes humorless daughter to a weaving contest. Yeah, Arachne clearly won, but when it's god vs. mortal . . . well, we play by different rules, man. Athena turned Arachne into a spindly spider and said, "I concede. You're the best spinner. *Now go spin, bitch!*"

Ares | *God of War*
Here's a guy who needs no introduction, even to mortals. If you're familiar with mass slaughter and bloody conquest, you know my boy Ares. He doesn't know the meaning of the word retreat—and I mean that literally. He has no idea. That goes for the word withdrawal as well, in all its denotations. He's the only guy I know who finds the Underworld boring because "you can't kill anyone there since they're already dead."

Argus | *Mortal Shipwright*
Inspired by Athena of course, this master shipbuilder designed and built the fabulous *Argo*, the first true longboat capable of navigating the high seas. Jason and his goofy crew of Argonauts sailed this vessel in search of the Golden Fleece. I'm thinking of having Argus invent the yacht next.

Arkas | *Mortal Founder of Arkadia*
Crazy story here. Arkas is . . . related to me. Okay, he's my son, courtesy of a great little Nymph named Kallisto. (Look her up in this roster if you want the sordid details.) A great hunter, Arkas went on to found Arkadia, a place that produced some of the best warriors on the planet. It eventually produced Atalanta herself—as impressive a mortal hero as you'll ever see.

Artemis | *Goddess of the Hunt*
Another daughter of mine, via Leto. Twin sister of Apollo, Artemis surpasses even her brother's prodigious skill with the bow and arrow. She loves wild animals and they seem to love her right back even though she slaughters them daily by the dozens. A lot of mountain Nymphs (like Kallisto) serve as her hunting attendants. Weirdly, she's a fanatical virgin, and demands vows of chastity from all her Nymphs as well. Where did that come from? Not my side of the family.

Atalanta | *Virgin Huntress Hero*
Daidalos has this gal nailed. His monument to her reads: "Stubborn Atalanta. First to strike and first to action." She's one of the truly great mortal heroes. I wish I could cook up a few more just like her!

Athena | *Goddess of Wisdom and Military Strategy*
Anybody who isn't familiar with the story of my daughter Athena doesn't deserve a Golden Isle tour package, in my opinion. The Grove of Kleos is her special region on Chryse.

Atlas | *Titan God of Astronomy*
This huge meathead fought with his loser Titan kin in the great war. As punishment, I hoisted the sky onto his shoulders and said, "Don't drop this! If you do, everybody dies, including you!"

Augeias | *Mortal King of Elis*
This rich bastard owned the biggest cattle herd in the Golden Isle. Thousands of animals, evacuating their massive bowels into their cavernous stables every day. But Augeias was so cheap he couldn't spare a few coins for a cleanup crew. When the wind blew the wrong direction, half of Greece gagged. King Eurystheus was so disgusted that he added "clean the Augean Stables" to the list of labors he assigned to Herakles. The big guy had to reroute a couple of rivers through the stables to complete the task!

Battus | *Limestone Snitch*
When Hermes stole Apollo's prized cattle, a shepherd named Battus witnessed the deed, so Hermes paid him to keep silent. But then Hermes disguised himself, returned to Battus, and offered a cash reward for info as a test. When Battus pointed out the hiding spot, Hermes turned the rat into a limestone statue.

Baukis | *Mortal Peasant Wife*

Why put some old crone in this roster, you ask? Answer: Because she's *hospitable*.

Bellerophon | *Mortal Horse Whisperer*

This is the guy who tamed and rode Pegasos. What a feat! Of course, he couldn't have done it without a charmed bridle from Athena, but it's still impressive. Man and horse rode around for years doing heroic tasks. Unfortunately, Bellerophon got arrogant and tried to ride Pegasos up to Mount Olympos. I blasted him off the horse and the long fall crippled him for life.

Boreas | *God of the Frigid North Wind*

Very strong god, violent temper. When Boreas gets drunk at dinner parties he staggers around, bellowing: "I am the bringer of winter!" Nobody likes him. He thinks goose down is a conspiracy against his powers. However, his new cologne line, the North Wind, is some real nose candy.

Brontes | *Cyclopic Blacksmith*

Known as "Brontes the Bright" . . . which is hilarious if you happen to know the one-eyed dolt. He and his equally dim brother Steropes labor in the great forges as assistants to my son, the smith-god Hephaistos.

Cassiopeia | *Mortal Queen of Aethiopia*

This foolish woman boasted that her daughter Andromeda was more beautiful than Poseidon's Nereid daughters. What a joke! Have you ever seen the Nereid synchronized swim team? You won't find creatures more gorgeous.

Centaurs | *Legendary Equine-ish Creatures*

Half man, half horse, all party animal! These hybrid wild folk gallop around harmlessly until you give them a drink. Then they start rearing up and looking for things to mount.

Cerberos | *Three-Headed Hound of Hades*

Make sure your Chryse Island tour guide takes you past the huge scary Cerberos heads carved from the rocks in the Grove of Kleos region. The kids will love it! This ugly canine monstrosity was the guard dog of Hades and his Underworld. Its capture was the final labor of Herakles assigned by King Eurystheus.

◇ ◇ ◇

Charon | *Ferryman of Styx*

What a job *this* guy has! He ferries all souls of the newly deceased across the River Styx into the Underworld, and gets a gold coin per corpse! These Coins of Charon are very valuable indeed. Charon is a stunningly grim dude, a perfect match for his chosen career path.

Circe | *Sea Sorceress*

Everybody knows that my niece Circe whips up the meanest magic potions in the known cosmos, right? Daughter of Poseidon, she's the dark beauty who hilariously turned Odysseus's crew into pigs. She changed them back eventually, but only after Odysseus agreed to sleep with her. I like a woman who knows how to get what she wants. Like Aphrodite . . . or Hera.

Cretan Bull | *Divine Bovine Sign*

When Minos ascended to the throne in Crete, he asked for a sign from Poseidon to confirm his rightful position as king. In response, the sea god sent Minos a snow-white bull, asking only that the creature be sacrificed to him in return. But this Cretan Bull was so magnificent that Minos instead hid it among his royal herds. Angry as hell, Poseidon directed Aphrodite to curse Minos's wife with lust for the great bull so she would mate with it. This bizarre union produced the Minotaur of Crete—half man, half raging bull. (Surely it also triggered some intense marital therapy.) Later, Herakles was tasked with capturing that same Cretan Bull as the seventh in his series of labors for King Eurystheus. Minos was happy to help, thrilled to have Herakles wrangle his wife's snorting lover away from Crete.

Cyclops | *Monstrous One-Eyed Goon*

If you don't know what a Cyclops is, you've been living under a rock for a few centuries. I will say this: you really don't want one of these guys "keeping an eye on you." It's a truly unsettling experience. It doesn't help that its single eye is about the size of a midsized chariot rental. Ever seen a Cyclops cry? That's something you can't ever really unsee, trust me. I bet they'd make good private investigators, though. Also, I have to admit, a couple of them ended up as excellent blacksmiths. A Cyclops actually crafted my all-powerful thunderbolt, if can you believe it.

Daphne | *Tragically Innocent Naiad*

This freshwater Nymph, daughter of the river god Peneus, dedicated herself to virginity at a very young age. One sad day my son Apollo ran into Daphne at a deserted spring just as Eros nicked him with one of his love arrows. Apollo fell hopelessly for Daphne and chased her around for a few days, or maybe it was weeks, I don't really recall. (If you're thinking No Means No and #MeToo, you're exactly right.) And it gets worse. The poor girl finally jumped in her dad's river and begged him for help. Unfortunately, the best thing Peneus (who's none too sharp) could come up with was . . . turn her into a laurel tree. Nice move, P. You couldn't just put her up in an Athens condo until you got a restraining order? As a result, Apollo now has a possibly unhealthy obsession with laurel wreaths. In any case, if your Golden Isle tour takes you into the Valley of Eternal Spring, be sure to check out the Apollo and Daphne statue that Daidalos commissioned.

Deimos | *Demonic God of Dread*

Son of Ares and Aphrodite, Deimos has one simple job. Before any battle, he sneaks through enemy ranks to spread grisly, terrifying rumors about his dad, thus paralyzing foes with dread. (Oddly enough, most of the rumors are true.) Once the fighting starts, Deimos hops in the lead chariot with twin brother Phobos—another truly creepy kid—and howls like a lunatic, sending fear rippling through enemy ranks. I'll be honest, it sounds like a lot of fun.

Demeter | *Goddess of Agriculture*

Very touchy woman, Demeter. Once she was wandering around Attika tired and thirsty when a guy named Misme offered her a drink. She downed it so fast that Misme's son laughed, so she turned the kid into a lizard: "Thanks for the drink, and here's a little something for your terrarium!" She's my older sister . . . although I didn't really meet Demi until Dad regurgitated her when I was a boy. Later, she and I had a thing—yeah, Persephone is our kid. (I told you we gods have a lot of "crossover" issues.)

Dionysos | *God of the Grape Harvest and Ritual Insanity*

I'm not one to party with my kids, but Di is a maniac. Seriously, if you're looking for a good time, Dionysos is your go-to guy for drunken frenzy. His main gig is getting people to shed inhibitions, often with a little help from the age-old processes of fermentation, aging, and clarification—the kid really knows his grape clusters. His vintages are legendary. To his many cult followers, wine with revelry is a deeply religious experience. Amen to that.

Drakon Ismenios | *Mighty Serpent Monster*

If you do any hiking in the War's Den region of Chryse, you'll likely come across the massive, sun-bleached skeleton of a mighty serpent monster, the Drakon Ismenios. In its heyday, this thing was the beloved pet of Ares, God of War. Its teeth had a really eerie magic—if you knocked one out and it fell to the ground, a powerful Spartoi soldier would immediately sprout from the spot. This was fun to do because the Spartoi would look around blinking and say, "Wasn't I just chewing something?"

Dryads | *Tree Nymphs*

These shy acolytes of Artemis can shape shift from Nymph to tree and back at will. You always want a few of these gals at your autumn fertility party, if possible. When the leaves start dropping, look out! Originally the spirits of oaks, Dryads eventually evolved into other tree varieties as well. They live only as long as the trees they inhabit . . . but then, some trees live hundreds and even thousands of years.

Echo | *Mountain Nymph . . . Mountain Nymph . . . Mountain Nymph*

Confession here: I used this young Oread to distract Hera whenever I fooled around with other Nymphs. Echo was such a brainless chatterbox, she could talk about anything—or more accurately, *nothing*—incessantly. Eventually, she annoyed Hera so much that my dear wife took away Echo's speech except the ability to repeat the last words of other speakers. (I really don't know what Hera was thinking here. It's more annoying than endless chatter.) To make matters worse, the poor Nymph spotted Narcissus in the woods one day and fell in hopeless love. Her "disorder" meant she couldn't tell the lad how she felt—not that it mattered, since the self-obsessed, onanistic little twit could only love himself anyway. Echo found this so crushing that she faded away into narrow canyons and really big empty ballrooms for a while. But I'm told she eventually managed to land a good job as a therapist. I hear she invented the art of active listening . . . and getting paid for it, also an art.

Endymion | *Sleeping Hunk of Shepherd*

This poor guy was a real looker. One day he napped in a cave on Mount Latmus and the moon goddess Selene wandered in looking for a clean restroom. Smitten at first sight, she begged me to cast a sleep spell on the guy so she could stare at him and, well, other stuff. Endymion never woke up, but Selene bore him fifty daughters. I have . . . no comment on this.

Ephialtes | *Giant Imbecile*

Along with his moronic brother Otos, this brawny giant crammed my hotheaded son Ares into a bronze pot, locked it shut, and then laid siege to Mount Olympos. Things were touch and go against the monsters for a while—they're both *really, really* big—but then my quick-witted daughter Artemis tricked the two dolts into spearing each other. Now *that* was funny.

◇ ◇ ◇

The Erinyes | *Chthonic Goddesses of Vengeance and Retribution*

Perhaps better known as the Furies, these are three supernasty goddesses, and please tell them I mean that in the most respectful way. They have a strict code of conduct, and if you break it, well, it's not pretty. The Erinyes punish crimes against the natural order by hounding transgressors relentlessly, shrieking day and night: *Don't kill your mother! Don't sleep with the babysitter! Never swear a false oath! Did you forget to floss again?* or whatever your thing was. It's harrowing, man.

Eris | *Goddess of Discord, Chaos, and Really Bad Decisions*

Eris takes great delight in the suffering of mortals. She also gets a kick out of turning gods against each other. Hence, nobody invites her to parties. She's nearly as universally despised as her son Ted Cruz, God of Obsequious Pusillanimity. Eris almost singlehandedly started the Trojan War! Everybody knows that story . . .

Eros | *God of Love, Sex, and Desire*

Son of Aphrodite, mischievous Eros is beloved by all . . . or by *most*, anyway. (It's possible his mischief may have spawned an enemy or two along the way.) This winged cherub flits around slinging his love arrows, inflicting the "delicious wounds" that make folks do crazy, giddy, even illicit things. Like, you know, adultery and whatnot. Or sex with bulls and swans. It's also said that Eros pioneered the use of blindfolds during foreplay, but that might just be something Hermes made up to rationalize his own preferences. Be sure to check out the fun constellation puzzle at Eros's Haven in the Valley of Eternal Spring, his mom's region of Chryse.

Erymanthos Boar | *Fearsome Tusk Monster*

Not to be confused with the Kalydonian Boar, this enormous, wild hog-beast usually roamed the sparsely populated foothills around Mount Erymanthos, hence its name. Unfortunately, sometimes the boar would lumber downhill and start tearing apart nearby farmlands, groves, and villages. All the locals, even the heroes, were scared to death. So, of course, King Eurystheus decided to make the boar's capture the fourth labor of Herakles—again, as with his other labor assignments, the king assumed the task was impossible.

But Herakles consulted his mentor, Chiron the Centaur, who suggested luring the boar into deep snow so it couldn't maneuver well. Then the two cracked open a huge amphora of killer wine—its fruity nose drew every other Centaur from miles around, and they all ended up getting hammered. What a night! Ten-furlong races, hoof boxing, arrows flying all over the place! The next day, a hungover Herakles staggered above the snowline of Mount Erymanthos, hogtied the immense boar, and carried it back to the royal court of Eurystheus. The king was so panicked by the creature's horrifying tusks and foaming jaws (not to mention the stench) that he hid inside an empty bronze jar and begged Herakles to get rid of it.

Europa | *Queen of Crete*

I swept this young woman off with me to Crete and made her queen of the island. It's a rough area so I commissioned a metallic protector-bot from my son Hephaistos. He crafted a powerful automaton named Talos who reported to Europa and patrolled the coastline, tossing boulders at brigand boats.

Eurynome | *Nymph of Water Meadows and Pasturelands*

Another daughter of Oceanos and Tethys, Eurynome was one of the elder Oceanids, the three thousand sisters who were all Nymphs inhabiting freshwater sources. Some have called her the "Nurse of Hephaistos" because she helped nurture and raise the fallen Hephaistos after his mother had tossed the infant from Mount Olympos down to the island of Lemnos, an impressive heave by any standards. I can vouch that nobody throws things quite like Hera.

Eurystheus | *Mortal King of Argos and Cousin of Herakles*

You'll see this guy's name mentioned a lot in this chapter. When a remorseful Herakles needed penance after killing his wife and kids, I remanded him to ten years of servitude under King Eurystheus of Argos, his cousin. Unfortunately, the king tried to take advantage of the situation by giving Herakles a list of twelve near-impossible tasks (all listed in the **Labors of Herakles** entry). But put an emphasis on the "near"—you could always count on Herakles to get the job done.

Gaia | *Mother Earth Goddess*

My grandmother Gaia is the most primordial deity of all, the mother of all life in the cosmos. She emerged first from the swirling soup, then birthed Ouranos. With Grandpappy on board, she *really* got to work, creating many primal creatures, including the Titans (including my mom Rhea and dad Kronos), as well as the Cyclopes, Hekatonchires, giants, Furies, and the earliest sea gods. Good lord, what a brood that must have been! Even Typhon claims to be their son.

Ganymede | *Ridiculously Gorgeous Trojan Prince*

This young man's beauty transcended gender and species and everything else, in my judgment. I once turned into an eagle and kidnapped him just to get some alone time. (Much drama ensued.) I was so smitten I sent Hermes to offer Ganymede's dad an entire herd of very god-quality horses in exchange for letting me keep his son in my retinue as a "cupbearer"—go ahead, cue the snickers. But the old guy was actually thrilled and proud of his boy. Of course, Hera wasn't happy about the deal, but even she ended up liking Ganymede, in a nasty begrudging sort of way. We immortalized him by turning him into the constellation Aquarius, the water bearer—in the sky right next to Aquila the Eagle.

Geryon | *Huge Giant with Cattle*

Here's one of those brutal twelve labors that King Eurystheus decreed his cousin Herakles had to perform as penance. Geryon was a truly huge giant—like, really *massively* colossal, so big and ugly you could mistake him for a two-mile stretch of badlands. (Some say Geryon actually had three heads and three sets of legs, all connected at the waist—although I never met the guy, so I can't confirm.) He owned a big herd of red cattle, and Eurystheus really wanted them. So, Herakles traveled to Geryon's grazing lands, shot an arrow into the giant's forehead, and then drove the cows back to his cousin's kingdom. Just like that. Lord, Herakles had even less of a conscience than I do.

Gorgon | *Dread Monster with Snaky Hair*

Once so rare even we gods thought they were just scary bedtime stories, Gorgons are hideous monsters with horrifying eye saucers and tangled hair made of living, venomous serpents. Where'd they come from? My guess is some stupid sorcerer got drunk—Orpheus, maybe—slung a spell at a snake, and accidentally zapped his angry wife too. Making eye contact with a Gorgon turns you into stone, so that theory makes sense to me. (You know, depending on the timing, getting petrified could be better than Viagra.) The most famous Gorgon is of course Medusa. (See **Medusa**.) She was so intense that her stony gazing thing still worked even after Perseus beheaded her!

Griffin | *Resplendent Eagle-Lion Creature*

This legendary, majestic flying beast has the body of a lion with the head and wings of an eagle, plus eagle talons on its front feet. *So* badass. Griffins mate for life—if one dies, the other lives out its life alone, never seeking another mate. That's proof right there that Griffins and gods come from entirely different realms of existence.

Hades | *God King of the Underworld*

One of my two brothers, Poseidon being the other. The three of us have our differences, but I think you'd have to say, when the chips are down, we're total bros. Hades is the grim one, of course—ruling the Underworld will flatten out your emotional affect. But pour a little Lethe water into him and things get interesting. He wraps his arm around my neck, knuckles my hair. Yeah, even though Sky and Underworld are such opposite realms, we have a bond I can't quite explain. I hear his gift to the Hall of the Gods can be fun to play with. Not sure what it does.

Harmonia | *Goddess of Harmony and Concord*

A few years ago, when my son Hephaistos figured out his wife Aphrodite was having an affair with my other son Ares, he was so livid he vowed to curse any child who might result from the infidelity. Guess who was born nine months later? Yeah, Harmonia—a super-nice kid, always resolving arguments between squabbling friends, writing up postwar peace treaties, stuff like that. Far as I can tell, her life is charmed. But unnamed sources with foresight tell me Hephaistos is just letting his vengeance stew . . . waiting for the right moment to unleash it on this really pleasant, innocent, precious, faultless young girl. (Heph's so much like his mother sometimes, it scares me.)

Harpies | *"Bird-Bodied, Girl-Faced Things"*

That's how Virgil describes them, anyway. (What, you think Apollo is the only god who can see the future?) He adds: "Their hands are talons, their droppings abominable, their faces haggard with hunger insatiable." Yeah, I can definitely second his take on the droppings—whatever these girls eat doesn't digest very well. A bunch of the vile, screeching pests have started flapping around the Golden Isle lately. I'm told they have a queen somewhere named Ozomene. She must be a real gem.

Helen of Troy | *Mortal It Girl*

Actually, she started out as Helen of Sparta, not Troy. Widely considered the most beautiful mortal woman in the world, Helen was the wife of King Menelaos, the Spartan ruler and a classic tough guy. But Aphrodite, in exchange for winning a pathetic vanity contest (see my **Eris** entry), arranged a meeting between Helen and Paris, Prince of Troy. Our favorite love goddess also sent her son Eros, who nailed Helen with an arrow so she went gaga for the trust-fund kid. Off they fled to Troy! An angry Menelaos followed. He brought Greece with him. The rest is history.

Helios | *Titan God of the Sun*

Reliable Helios hitches the sun to his flying chariot and hauls it across the sky, east to west, every day. Visitors should check out his gleaming island temple just off the northeast coast of the Forgelands.

Hephaistos | *God of the Forge*

My son Hephaistos is a brilliant master of metalwork, blacksmithing, forging, fires, sculpture, invention, crafting, masonry, all that stuff. Daidalos dedicated an entire region of Chryse to him: the Forgelands. He's a hands-on guy, right? We've never really talked much . . . perhaps understandable since his mom basically hammer-threw him off Mount Olympos when he was a toddler due to her embarrassment at his disfigured leg. But I tell you, he *really* plays up the whole introverted, tortured artist thing. The only topic that excites him is the malleability of adamantine. Athena tells me, "Dad, he's not a talker. Heph expresses himself through his work." Whatever. If he talked more, maybe his wife Aphrodite wouldn't cheat on him so much.

Hera | *Goddess of Jealousy*

Okay, maybe that's a little snarky—technically, she's goddess of "marriage and family," LOL. She's also my sister, my wife, queen of the gods, and mother of Hephaistos and Ares. Favorite animal: lion. Favorite traits: fidelity, monogamy. Favorite pastime: punishing adulterers. The woman is constantly in revenge mode because, well, I fool around a lot. But since I'm king of gods, she has to take out her jealous rages on my unfortunate consorts and assorted illegitimate children. Like Kallisto, for example—nice girl, fun in bed. Hera found out and turned her into a huge freaking bear. She also messed up Echo pretty bad. (See my **Echo** entry.) Leto got it good, too. Even though I'm immortal, I consider myself lucky to be alive. Amazingly, Hera has remained faithful to me all these years.

Herakles | *Mortal Hero of Legendary Strength*

This brutish beefcake is so famous some people think he's a god, which drives Hera nuts—she hates the guy. Sure, he slaughtered a *lot* of monsters . . . although in my opinion (which is divine, don't forget) some of his feats were a tad overhyped. Cerberos was tough, and the Nemean Lion was no patsy. But washing cow crap from a stable? Snagging a few apples? Scaring away birds with a rattle? Not exactly godlike. I will admit, though: in terms of sheer numbers, Herakles kicked a *lot* of ass. He's perhaps best known for the twelve ridiculously difficult tasks he performed as penance for King Eurystheus. (See my **Labors of Herakles** entry.) And the king was his cousin! Man, don't get me started about relatives. They can be the worst.

Anyway, Herakles had many flaws—he was too boastful, too proud, too angry all the time, drank too much, insulted too many people, cheated on his wives (one of whom he actually murdered while hexed with one of Hera's insanity curses). My god, he got drunk and started fights at *funerals*. What a hoot this guy was. I can honestly say I've never met anyone more entertaining than Herakles in my very long immortal life. It took a shirt smeared with Hydra venom to topple the great man.

Hermes | *God of Trickery and Herald of the Gods*

Ah, Hermes. My *colorful* son. Clever, impish, mischievous—a real pain in the ass. Always the snarky joke, the sly nod to irony or paradox. Sure, he has his uses. Without him, Ares would still be stuck in that stupid bronze pot. The winged sandals help in his day job at Mount Olympian Messenger Service, plus he moonlights as that guy in the Styx T-shirt who walks backward, guiding lost souls to the Underworld ferry: *This way, folks! Hands inside the railings, please! Be sure to check out the cafeteria and bookstore while you're here!* He's also quite the thief—I'm pretty sure Hermes has a secret stash of stolen gear somewhere on Chryse. He claims to regret escorting Pandora to earth per my request . . . where she unleashed such nasty torments from her box. (I know, I know—too easy.) Clearly, Hermes has a soft spot in his heart for mortals. Such easy marks.

Hippolyta | *Mortal Queen of the Amazons*
This fearsome female warrior led an entire tribe of assorted female warriors, the Amazons. Hippolyta's magic girdle famously boosted her combat skills, so King Eurystheus sent Herakles to acquire it.

Hydra of Lerna | *Water Monster*
Serpentine fiend with many heads. Killing this beast was the second labor assigned by King Eurystheus to Herakles.

Hygeia | *Goddess of Health, Cleanliness, and Ubiquitous Hand Sanitizer Stations*
Hygeia is super clean, which is great. Her scrub brush is certainly legendary, and everybody loves her moppy hair. But lately she's turned into this overbearing antigerm crusader. I think she just needs to meet someone. Maybe a nice partner who can help her explore the joys of being dirty.

Io | *Mortal Princess of Argos*
One of my favorite mortal consorts, Io was as spicy as a Greek peperoncino. We had a lot of fun roleplaying—she was a cow, I was a cloud. It got tricky because Io's day job in Argos was priestess in the Temple of Hera, my wife. We had a couple of kids together, but it got too complicated. Eventually I had to send her to Egypt, where she ended up dating a pharaoh, I believe.

Iolaos | *Mortal Nephew*
This nephew of the mighty Herakles drove his uncle's chariot whenever the big guy overimbibed, which was pretty much every weekend. He also helped Herakles complete a few of his labors—especially the second one, killing the many-headed Lernean Hydra. Years later, Iolaos became an Argonaut, but wasn't everybody? I swear, every résumé in Greece has "Argonaut" listed somewhere in its employment history.

Ixion | *Mortal King of the Lapiths*
When I invited this royal clown to visit my court on Mount Olympos, he tried to move on my wife, Hera, during a banquet! So I smote him good and strapped him to a flaming wagon wheel that I set spinning for all eternity.

Jason | *Mortal Leader of the Argonauts*
Born a prince of Iolcos, Jason was sent off at a young age to a centaur boarding school. There, he was raised by the wise centaur teacher Chiron. As a result, Jason grew up very well educated, although sometimes he'd snort and stamp his feet on the ground to count. A guy named Peleus had usurped the Iolcos throne from Jason's parents, but he promised to return Jason's inheritance if the young man could retrieve the legendary Golden Fleece, as Peleus wanted to upgrade his hiking apparel. Jason knew it would be a difficult task, so he hired the master shipwright Argus to build a decent longboat, and then recruited a crew of fifty heroes, give or take, plus

one barnacle scraper. The group included superstars like Atalanta, Herakles, Peleus, and a couple of winged Boreads for aerial reconnaissance and anti-Harpy ops. Jason and crew christened the ship the *Argo*, and thus called themselves the Argonauts. The *Argo* sailed to Kolkhis, where Jason completed three tasks for the local king (with the help of the king's lovestruck daughter, Medea) to earn the Golden Fleece.

Kadmos | *Mortal Founder of Thebes*

One of the truly great old-school adventurers, Kadmos is perhaps best known as the Greek entrepreneur who pulled off the Thebes startup . . . with the help of a few Spartoi soldiers born of dragon's teeth, an unsettling story if ever there was one. (Check out my **Drakon Ismenios** entry.) The Kadman can thank me for his brand—he never would have left home if I hadn't abducted his sister Europa. (Don't give me that look. It was an entirely *consensual* abduction, plus she ended up queen of Crete.) His search for Sis produced some really great tales. *You're welcome, pal.*

Kalliope | *Chief Muse*

Kalliope is the leader of the nine female muses who inspire art and music and poetry and other activities that drive sensitive mortals into poverty and drive their parents crazy. It's true! A lot of parents really hate Kalliope's gals, preferring instead the muses of medicine, law, and investment banking. Kids!

Kallisto | *Ursine Mountain Nymph*

This gal was one of my favorite consorts, maybe even number one. As an attendant of Artemis, Kallisto was big on the virginity thing. It took some of my best moves to dissuade her of that ridiculous notion. When Hera found out and turned Kallisto into a humongous bear, I felt so bad I tossed her into the northern sky where she twinkles eternally as Ursa Major.

Kalydonian Boar | *Scourge of Artemis*

One autumn, King Oeneus of Kalydon made a terrible mistake. During his kingdom's annual harvest festival, he neglected to offer a sacrifice to the goddess Artemis. Arty doesn't take snubs well (as I've learned the hard way), and she responded to this insult by unleashing a monstrous wild boar upon Kalydon. The ravenous beast devoured crops, tore apart vineyards, and terrorized the kingdom's rural villages. Oeneus put out an urgent call for skilled hunters to slay the boar. Many renowned Greek heroes responded, and an all-star hunting party began tracking the fearsome animal. But it was an arrow from the bow of Atalanta that finally pierced the hide of the Kalydonian Boar, drawing first blood. That moment was the starting point of her fame.

Kassandra | *Trojan Priestess of Apollo*

The curse on this poor Trojan priestess became legendary. It started with some fairly egregious workplace harassment. Kassandra's boss in the city's Temple of Apollo—that's right, it was Apollo himself— kept following her around, grabbing her ass, trying to seduce her. He even gave her the gift of prophecy, but she still rebuffed him. Now, once you bestow a gift of prophecy, you can't take it back, not even if the one bestowing that gift is the God of Prophecy himself. Thus, Apollo got upset (in his totally chill Apollonian sort of way) and added a curse to the gift. Going forward, Kassandra could indeed see the future. *But nobody would ever believe her.* The diabolical genius of this curse still takes my breath away.

Poor Kassandra eventually went mad, and became a figure of epic tragedy. And it just gets worse for the girl after that. When Troy fell and was sacked—which she totally foresaw, even though everybody replied, "Are you on drugs? Trojans never lose. Shut up, Kassandra!"—a Greek warrior broke into a temple where she hid and violated her. Then she got thrown into the entourage of that hairy clown, Agamemnon, who made her his concubine and dragged her back to Greece. When he got home, his wife's lover murdered both of them.

Kedalion | *Apprentice of Hephaistos*

This plucky demigod was Hephaistos's most reliable assistant and one heck of an ore smelter, I'm told. When the lunkhead hunter Orion tried to molest a king's daughter and got stabbed in the eyes for it, he managed to stumble blindly to Heph's forge in Lemnos. There,

Kedalion got assigned to sit on Orion's shoulders and guide him eastward to the Temple of Helios for healing. Don't miss the big statue depicting this hilarious trek in the Forgelands!

Kottos the All-Seeing | *Monster with a Hundred Hands (Give or Take)*

Kottos is one of the legendary Hekatonchires monsters, the gruesome giant "Hundred-Handers" who helped me overthrow the Titans, and who now guard the Tartaros exit so the losers can't escape. Some call Kottos the ultimate abomination, but not me. I call him "boss." As long as a horrifying monster is on your side, don't provoke him. It's like, "Keep an eye on these gates, will you, boss? We don't want any Titans getting out!" Because of his job, I don't think you'll see Kottos anywhere on the Golden Isle. But just in case, remember this: the guy has the most heinous forward roll attack I've ever seen!

Kronos | *King of the Titan Gods*

Years of therapy have taught me that every family is different, and one shouldn't be quick to judge the dynamics of familial interrelationships. But my dad Kronos was a sick paranoid bastard, no question. If I hadn't smote and shackled him in the deepest fetid pit of Tartaros to suffer excruciating torment for all eternity, he might have done some real, lasting damage to people's feelings up here on Olympos. Look, the guy bought into some crackpot conspiracy theory that one of his kids would depose him, so he ate all of us . . . well, except me, thanks to quick thinking by my mom, Rhea. To be fair to Kronos, it wasn't a *totally* crazy response. Sometimes you have to be proactive about prophecies, get out ahead of the opinion curve, I realize that. I've had consultants tell me that many times. But Dad took

it to a whole new, weird, overreactive level. I'm told he even salted Demeter before swallowing her. That's demented! I had to act fast to save my siblings, my family. Plus, Kronos was a big roadblock in my vertical path to omnipotent rule. By deposing him, I made life better for all of us, especially me. My people all agree it was a win-win move.

Kyknos | *Murderous Son of Ares*

This kid was about as psychotic as they come. Hard to believe he's my grandson. My god, he built temples out of innocent people's bones! Thank god Herakles finally kicked his ass. Kyknos's mother was mortal, so maybe that explains it. And, well . . . Ares is his dad. Okay, the more I think about it, the more it makes sense.

Lernean Hydra | *Many-Headed Lake Monster*

Some say this smelly beast (its scent could literally kill you) was yet another spawn of Typhon, which certainly makes sense. The foul thing was finally killed by Herakles because I was pretty busy that weekend. And yes, killing the Hydra was yet another labor of Herakles assignment from King Eurystheus.

Lykaon | *Mortal King of Arcadia*

This madman tried to serve his charbroiled son to me at a feast, so I turned the guy into a werewolf. When the moon is full, you can hear Lykaon out in the woods, howling about government spending. Island tourists should look for the commemorative fresco puzzle that Daidalos installed up on King's Peak.

Marsyas | *Satyr Aulete*

This is the aulos-playing Satyr who challenged Apollo to a musical duel. As Apollo is God of Music, it was not a bright plan. Funny thing, though—Marsyas was indeed the better musician. But Apollo won anyway because his sister Athena judged the contest. Then Apollo had the happy, talented fellow flayed alive for challenging a god.

Medea | *Sorceress and Fleece Enabler*

This enchantress was daughter of Aeetes, king of Kolkhis. When Jason and his Argonauts arrived to pilfer the Golden Fleece, Medea fell hard for the handsome captain. She helped Jason complete her father's ridiculous tasks, then ran off with him to Iolcos on the *Argo* (his boat).

Medusa | *Most Infamous Gorgon*

One of three monstrous Gorgon sisters (see my **Gorgon** entry), Medusa had snakes for hair and a gaze that, if you met it, turned you to stone. After the Greek hero Perseus beheaded her, Medusa's amazing head lived on—he used its stony gaze as a weapon to petrify foes. Eventually Perseus gave the head as an offering to Athena.

Menelaos | *Mortal King of Sparta*

This notorious hothead somehow reeled in Helen, the hottest girl by far in Greece, to be his queen. Of course, life in Sparta is pretty stripped down. Helen wasn't exactly pampered or awash in luxury. So, when Paris of Troy came to visit, she was already primed to scoot. Then Eros shot her with an arrow, and off she fled with the pretty boy. An angry Menelaos rallied his Spartan troops, called his Greek allies to join him, scrounged together about a thousand transport ships, and sailed after the little minx. To make a long story short, he won, happily watched Philoctetes slay Paris, sacked Troy, took Helen back home, and they lived spartanly ever after.

Metis | *River Nymph*

This is my first ex-wife—so cunning and intelligent, traits she passed on to our daughter, Athena. Metis is the one who whipped up the special potion that my mom and I fed my dad, Kronos, so he'd spew out all of my siblings.

Midas | *King with Golden Touch*

This is the famous guy that got a wish granted from Dionysos, making everything he touched turn to gold—furniture, people, food. Poor guy nearly starved to death before he got the wish reversed. He was a big fan of Pan's flute music, but in his old age he grew so sensitive to sound that he invented mufflers.

Mimas | *Giant Pain in the Ass*

Mimas was a powerful leader of the Gigantes brutes who tried to assault Mount Olympos and depose the rule of gods. Hephaistos threw molten iron in his face to end the threat. Boy, that's gotta hurt.

Minos | *Mortal King of Crete*

Look, I told you all about this guy way back in the first chapter, **Welcome to the Golden Isle!** Go back there now to recall what you've forgotten about Minos and his nasty little Minotaur problem. Mortals know how to turn pages, right? You do realize they're numbered in order? I invented that system. I also invented breathing. I tried to make it work underwater, but too many people drowned.

The Moirai | *Infallible Goddesses of Mortal Destiny*

Also known as "the Fates," these three regal goddesses are my daughters who control the life and destiny of every mortal. Their decisions are so final that even the gods must accept them, no questions asked.

Myrmex | *Insectile Plagiarist*

This woman was one of Athena's favorite temple acolytes until she tried to take credit for inventing the plow, saying she came up with it instead of Athena. How many times do I have to say it? When mortals try to claim godlike powers, bad things happen, e.g., Myrmex is an ant now, and none of the other ants go to hill parties.

Narcissus | *Mortal Self-Lover*

This lovely young fellow was actually quite a good hunter, though nobody really remembers that. Narcissus was a looker, pure and simple. Never seen a fairer complexion, thicker eyebrows, or more self-regard in anyone, god or mortal. Lots of people binary, nonbinary, trinary, Nymph—fell hard for him at first sight. But the first time Narcissus caught sight of his own reflection in a pool? Yeah, after that, nobody else measured up. He rejected all romantic advances, preferring to stare at himself all day. Somebody named a really nasty personality disorder after him. One can only hope mortals will never choose a leader afflicted with it.

Nemean Lion | *Toothy Tormentor of Argos*

Sent by Hera (who has a thing for lions) to terrorize the wooded hills of Nemea near Argos, this foul creature was said to be the offspring of Typhon himself. Killing this lion was the first labor assigned to Herakles during his period of penance and service to King Eurystheus.

Nereids | *Sea Nymphs*

These daughters of Poseidon are notoriously beautiful and have great voices with perfect pitch to boot. As prominent members of their dad's entourage, Nereids are super loyal to the sea king. In fact, they're the only ones entrusted to carry his trident, and right there is an obvious joke I'm not touching.

Nike | *Goddess of Victory*
This upbeat, trim-ankled beauty joined my Olympian team early during our war with the Titans, so she's a longtime ally. Nike is my divine charioteer, flying around the battlefield to reward victors with glory and fame—*swooshing* here, *swooshing* there. She works particularly well with Athena. What a duo! I'm fond of Nike, but truth be told, she sometimes goes to pieces under pressure.

Oceanids | *Goddesses of Springs and Fountains*
These three thousand daughters of Tethys and Oceanos inhabit the world's freshwater springs gushing up from the earth. They literally do nothing except sit there, bubbling. They do have effervescent personalities, though. Always good for a quick soak and massage! Although now that I think of it, my first wife, Metis, was an Oceanid. After I impregnated her . . . this may sound strange . . . she turned herself into a fly and so I ate her. It was a dick move, I admit. I paid for it because I had to birth the baby myself, right out of my forehead. (That kid was Athena, by the way.)

Oceanos | *Titan God of the Great River*
This damp fellow inhabits the enormous river that encircles the entire world. Homer calls him "deep flowing," which, apparently, is some kind of compliment. Even though Oceanos is a Titan, he refused to fight in the Titan war against us Olympian gods. So, after tossing all the other Titans down the hatch into Tartaros, I let Oceanos keep flowing around up here, doing his thing. He married Tethys and had six thousand kids. Can you imagine? *"Mom, Asterodia is mimicking me again!"* times six thousand. They took a family vacation here on Chryse a few weeks ago and I think the maintenance staff is still cleaning up.

Odysseus | *Mortal Hero and Famous Lost Guy*
One of my favorite mortals of all time, this guy. King of Ithica, known for his cunning, Odysseus led his Greek troops to Troy and proved a brilliant general in the field. But here's the best thing: *the whole Trojan Horse scam was his idea!* Sneakiest move of all time—and coming

from me, that's high praise. Even Hermes was impressed. Anyway, long journey home, never wavered, won back the heart of wife Penelope, *blah blah blah*, happy ending. Impressive stuff all around.

Oeneus | *Mortal King of Kalydon*
Here's a cautionary tale, folks. File it under "Gods Have Feelings Too." Oeneus was the entirely forgettable ruler of a lovely but largely insignificant land called Kalydon. One year, King Oeneus forgot to give the goddess Artemis a shout-out at his annual harvest rites, so she sent a gigantic, terrifying hog monster to ravage the kingdom. Poor Oeneus had to summon a bunch of mortal heroes (including the great Atalanta, one of my favorites) to save his domain from what came to be known as the Kalydonian Boar.

Orestes | *Famous Mortal Defendant*
His dad, King Agamemnon, fought for a glorious decade in the Trojan War. But when the king returned home in triumph, his wife's lover cut his throat. In revenge, Orestes killed the murderer, which was cool with everyone. But he also killed his mom. This violation of primal law got the terrifying Erinyes (AKA the Furies) on his tail, but good Athena called for justice and a trial of twelve judges. In the end, their vote set Orestes free. He thanked Athena and had a nice fruit basket delivered.

Orion | *Mortal Huntsman and Serial Sex Offender*
Orion was one of the most toxically masculine hunting enthusiasts ever. He thought he was a lady-slayer too, never taking no for an answer. But after he forced himself on the daughter of King Oenopion, the king's men blinded Orion and threw him into the woods. The big lout managed to stumble to Lemnos where Hephaistos's servant Kedalion guided him to the Temple of Helios for healing. In the end, Scorpio stung the guy to death and I tossed both (lout and scorpion) up into the sky as constellations.

Otos | *Giant Moron*
Along with his moronic brother Ephialtes, this brawny giant crammed my hotheaded son Ares into a bronze pot, locked it shut, and then laid siege to Mount Olympos. Things were touch and go against the monsters for a while—they're both *really, really* big—but then my quick-witted daughter Artemis

tricked the two dolts into spearing each other. Now *that* was comical.

And yes, I cut and pasted this from the **Ephialtes** entry, except I changed "funny" to "comical." Go ahead, sue me for plagiarizing myself. I dare you.

Ouranos | *God of the Sky*

Far as I can tell, my grandpappy Ouranos didn't do much except hover up there in his sky, keeping an eye on things, like a surveillance chopper. Well, I guess he did lock away most of the Cyclopes so they couldn't overthrow him according to a prophecy he'd heard. Oh, and he also tossed that big pearl into the sea, the one that foamed up and turned into Aphrodite. (Afterward he always spoke in this weird, really high-pitched voice.) Such a great story! And speaking of prophecy, here's a good one: Apollo's oracles tell me that, in the future, the Roman mispronunciation of grandpappy's name— Uranus—used in absolutely any sentence in a classroom would elicit more giggling than even audible flatulence. *Can we mine Uranus for minerals? Can I see Uranus at night?* What a legacy!

Ozomene the Hurricane | *The Harpy Queen*

Half avian raptor, half crazy-woman, filthy talons, so much shrieking, what a treat. In my experience (which is vast), anyone who takes a scary nickname like "the Hurricane" suffers from a crippling inferiority complex. I'm told all Harpies are possibly daughters of Typhon, the one guy who gets on my nerves even worse than bad poetry. Athena tells me Ozomene has an unhealthy fixation with Nike, goddess of victory. We think she's recruiting for her precision flying team, the Blue Harpies.

Pan | *God of Nature, Fertility, and Rustic Music*

This flea-bitten son of Hermes writes songs and prances around on his goat legs all day, looking for hookups. It's embarrassing, really. They named the pan flute after him. Whenever I hear it, I swear I start to itch. You know, Ares always wanted Pan to write him a God of War battle hymn. Who wants a battle hymn that sounds like a bunch of bleating? Plus, he overcharges.

Pandora | *Mortal Woman 1.0*

This gal was my first design of a mortal woman, so please cut me some slack. At the time, I was irritated with Prometheus for giving fire to mortal men. So, I sent Pandora down with a nice little boxed gift. Inside, I placed a lovely floral arrangement plus every horrible plague now known to mankind.

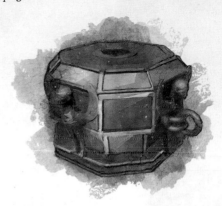

Paris | *Mortal Trojan Lightweight*

Okay, maybe the designation above is a bit harsh, but Paris was no hero—not in my book, anyway (and this is my book). True, I slyly appointed the punk to award the Apple of Discord to whoever was "fairest" among the goddesses Hera, Aphrodite, and Athena—a deadly task if ever there was one. Aphrodite bribed Paris with the love of Helen of Sparta, number one on the Hottest Mortals list . . . and so the kid tossed the Apple to Aphy. But then the smitten Paris abducted Helen from Sparta and whisked her off to his crib back in Troy. This launched a thousand ships and split our god ranks— some went pro-Greek, some pro-Trojan. The whole war was a joke, really—but in its course, Paris killed the most magnificent warrior I've ever known, Achilles, with a lucky arrow to the heel.

Pegasos | *Divine Winged Horse*

This flying stallion, graceful and gleaming white, is the offspring of Poseidon and Medusa. (*That's* a wild story I'll share over drinks sometime.) Pegasos is immortal but you rarely see the godly steed—he keeps to himself, tired of all the cowboys who keep trying to get famous by mounting him. The only one who ever succeeded was a guy named Bellerophon.

Penelope | *Mortal Good Wife*

Married to crafty Odysseus, king of Ithaca, this amazing woman waited twenty long years for her husband to return from the Trojan War. That kind of fidelity is inconceivable to me and probably deserves an award. Penelope was an attractive person *and* a wealthy queen, and so many, many suitors sought her hand during those two decades. But she fended them off, sometimes in really clever ways. Like husband, like wife, I guess.

Persephone | *Queen Goddess of the Underworld*
I told you I have a lot of kids. This daughter came courtesy of a wild night with Demeter. (I don't remember any of it.) When she was young, Persephone had a thing for Adonis (hey, who didn't?) and squabbled with Aphrodite over him. But I let my brother Hades abduct Persephone during a flower-picking field trip—a nice touch in my view, because she's also Goddess of Spring and Nature. He took his ill-gotten bride down to the Underworld where she reigns as his queen today. I hear Persephone hates the gig but stays for the pomegranate seeds. Whatever works.

Perseus | *Mortal Slayer of Monsters*
This guy is a straight-up badass. I'm a real fan. He slew a lot of monsters, but none more hideous and frightening than Medusa the Gorgon, the crazy snake-haired wench whose eye contact turned people to stone.

Phaethon | *Mortal Slayer of Monsters*
This kid was the son of Helios who kept pestering his dad to borrow the family sun chariot to impress his dimwitted layabout pals. Helios finally relented, a big mistake. As things went haywire and threatened to incinerate the entire freaking mortal world, I had to take executive action with extreme prejudice.

Philemon | *Mortal Peasant Geezer*
This is the "decrepit husband" of Baukis. I'll tell you all about them later on.

Phobos | *Demonic God of Panic and Fleeing*
Along with his equally disturbing twin brother, Deimos, Phobos is the son of Ares and Aphrodite. Not too surprising that the offspring of Love and War might be a little psycho, right? As adjutant to Ares, Phobos drives Daddy's chariot around enemy ranks on the battlefield spreading fear, panic, and the urge to run away shrieking. A pretty sweet gig, I'd say.

Polyphemos the Enraged | *Super-Ugly Cyclopic Monster*
If you're touring the Forgelands region of Chryse, you might want to keep an eye out (just one, ha ha ha!) for Polyphemos. I know it's not politically correct to imply that all Cyclopes are hideously repulsive, so let's just say, thank god he keeps his helmet on 24/7. As his formal title implies, he has some really serious anger management issues. (You probably would too if Odysseus stabbed out your one good eye.) He also eats people. I mean, like, *chews* and *digests*. It's disgusting—sure, gods swallow folks too, but we almost always hork them back up within a few weeks. They come out whole and good to go! No such luck with Polyphemos the One-Eyed Masticator.

Poseidon | *God of the Sea and Tectonic Mayhem*
Yes, he's my older sibling. Impressive guy, *huge* trident . . . they don't call him "earth shaker" for nothing. After my brothers and I overthrew our father, Kronos, we cast lots to split up the inheritance—I got the sky, Hades the Underworld, and Poseidon the seas. I think he feels shortchanged sometimes. "It's all tentacles and drama down here," he tells me. I tell him, "Hey, take a vacation! Use my temple! I got a nice pool!" But he has zero interest in the Golden Isle. You won't see him around here much.

Potamoi | *Gods of Rivers and Streams*
These three thousand sons of Tethys and Oceanos inhabit the world's moving waterways. You can't really miss them when they rise up and walk around in their personal animal forms. Some are bulls with man heads; others are men with bull heads; and a few just take on the sad shape of used-chariot salesmen.

Prometheus | *Titan God of Fire and Foresight*
Foresight? Really? This genius had the uncanny prescience to back the Titans in their pathetic losing war against us Olympians. Then he snuck into my condo, stole my fire, and gave it to mortals so they could develop (try not to laugh) "civilization." I guess Prometheus didn't quite *foresee* his punishment for this treachery. But Chryse visitors can see it every freaking day—just point a spyglass up the mountain at the guy chained to a rock. Don't do it right before lunch, though. Actually, maybe not right after lunch, either.

Psykhe | *Eventual Goddess of the Soul*
Born mortal, Psykhe grew into such a beautiful woman that her looks rivaled those of Aphrodite herself! Not

good for Psykhe, of course—Aphrodite wanted to kill her, preferably in a grotesquely inhumane way. But someone (probably Hermes) talked Aphy into sending her son Eros down to snipe Psykhe with one of his love arrows, timing it so the poor mortal girl would fall for the nearest hideous smelly beast. Hilariously, just before firing, Eros accidentally nicked himself with the arrow . . . and thus he fell madly in love with Psykhe! The kids eventually got married and wow, what a wedding feast. I gave Psykhe a sip of ambrosia so she could join Eros in immortality. They became quite the celebrity couple.

Rhea | *Titaness Mother of the Gods*

Hey, that's my mom! Titan goddess of fertility, motherhood, and birth, she coupled with Kronos to produce my sisters Hestia, Demeter, and Hera; my brothers Hades and Poseidon; and then me, the youngest. Good old psycho dad swallowed all five of my older siblings, trying to dodge the prophecy that one of his kids would overthrow him. So, when I was born, Mother hid me away on Crete. Then she wrapped up a big stone, pretended it was me, and handed it to Pops. You'd think old Kronos might want at least one kid to chuck thunderbolts with, but no, he just gulped the swaddled stone without even looking. After I grew into boyhood, we slipped dad an emetic and he promptly disgorged the rest of my family. We still laugh about it at family reunions.

Roe the Great | *Mythical Creature*

This great beast has never been encountered, but it is reputed to have the head of a lion and the body of a lion, though not the same lion.

Scorpio | *Scorpion-Shaped Bunch of Stars*

Orion, son of Poseidon, was a really huge guy and a great hunter—like, viciously good. His favorite hunting partner was Artemis, which made her twin brother Apollo jealous for some reason about which I choose not to speculate. Apollo conspired to create a giant scorpion that he named Scorpio. (I guess he thought leaving off the "N" would throw the homicide detectives off the trail.) He planted the deadly arachnid in Orion's favorite hunting glade, where it promptly stung the poor fellow to death. In memory of this largely inconsequential event, I tossed both of them up into my sky to become constellations. You can look up there for the Hunter and

the Scorpion every night, if you're bored and really have nothing better to do.

Selene | *Loony Goddess of the Moon*

This freaky deity fell in love with a pretty shepherd named Endymion while watching him sleep! She asked me to make the kid sleep eternally so she could "watch" him forever. Yeah, right. She *watched* him. That's why they ended up with fifty kids even though he never woke up.

Shades | *Incorporeal Minions*

These murky ghosts risen from the Underworld can be real pests. It is said they wander in aimless packs with no purpose until they find a Wraith—a former mortal hero, now corrupted. Then they all follow the Wraith. Like, everywhere. If Wraiths ever need to use a restroom, the Shade entourage just troops in behind and hangs out by the sink, cracking jokes.

Sisyphos | *Devious King of Corinth*

This mortal monarch annoyed me plenty during his life. But after he died he pulled a *really* irritating stunt, pranking Thanatos and sneaking back to the living. When we finally incarcerated his soul in Tartaros I dreamt up a great punishment. Sisyphos has to push a big rock uphill that rolls back down just as he reaches the top, every time, for all eternity. Ha!

Skamander | *Touchy River God*

This son of the Titan water deities Oceanos and Tethys took insults way too personally. When Achilles made fun of him on the killing fields outside Troy, the guy went totally psycho and started slinging huge waves of himself (he's a river god) at the Greek hero to drown him. Hephaistos had to step in and mediate with a blazing inferno that boiled away the water.

Steropes | *Another Cyclopic Blacksmith*

Along with his brother Brontes, Steropes forms the executive staff working under Hephaistos at the Forge of the Gods. I know these Cyclops siblings are smithy masters responsible for legendary gear like my own thunderbolts . . . but whenever Steropes ogles me, I just want to pluck that eye and donate it to a summer soccer camp!

Talos | *Bronze Coast Guard*

When I installed my consort Europa as queen of Crete, I asked my son Hephaistos to build a big metal goon to guard the island. He smelted up a bronze monster named Talos, and we deployed the big guy to patrol the Cretan coast. He was super tough but had a heel problem that drained all his juices.

Tantalus | *Wicked Mortal King*

To be honest, I don't really remember exactly what this guy did. I know I invited him to sit at my table once on Olympos, a rare privilege. Did he steal ambrosia? Or maybe he was the anonymous source in that nasty media exposé about our Olympian game design studio, Naughty Gods. Whatever it was, I cast him down into Tartaros. There, I left him starving and parched with thirst, standing in a pool of water with a fruit tree just overhead. *Ha ha ha!* If Tantalus bends to drink, the water recedes. If he tries to grab fruit, the tree rises up, just out of reach. I could watch for hours. But I tell you, I can never look at this guy without staring at his narrow little eyebrows—seriously, it's like somebody drew them with a Micron ultrathin graph pencil.

Tethys | *Titan Goddess of Fresh Water*

This unbelievably fertile gal married Oceanos, the Titan god who inhabits the great primordial river that encircles the world. Together, they produced six thousand children! No wonder those two were always bickering. Hera had to go mediate. She said all the screaming kids made it impossible to think straight around that house. Half are the Potamoi boys, most of whom got good-paying jobs as gods of the world's rivers and streams. (A few ended up working as sewage flows—isn't that every parent's nightmare?) The other three thousand kids are the Oceanid sisters, all Nymphs inhabiting springs, fountains, ponds, and those recirculating water-wall sculptures you see in shopping malls.

Thanatos | *God of Death*

This winged minion has one simple job. He greets souls of the newly deceased and escorts them down to their eternal dwelling place in the Underworld. We give everybody name tags so it's impossible to screw up. And yet, souls end up missing, or shipped off to entirely different mythologies. I probably need to consult with my HR hiring people.

Themis | *Goddess of Divine Justice . . . and Prophecy*

My second ex-wife perfectly embodies fairness, law, justice, and the divine order of things. Daidalos built a really nice Shrine of Themis on Chryse. Check it out! She certainly deserves it.

Theseus | *Mortal Athenian Hero*

Great slayer of odious ogres and hideous beasts, Theseus is probably best known as the hero who killed the man-eating Minotaur, although he also had a really nice little souvlaki stand near the Parthenon. Back in my **Welcome to the Golden Isle!** chapter I told you all about the Labyrinth that Daidalos built to imprison the Minotaur under the palace of King Minos in Crete. What I didn't tell you is that later, Theseus went to Crete, descended into the maze, and slew the great monster. Such a stud.

Thetis | *Kindly Sea Goddess*

This spritely sea Nymph, one of fifty sea Nymph sisters, lived on the volcanic island of Lemnos in her youth.

When Hera coldly tossed our lame son Hephaistos off Mount Olympos, Thetis and her friend Eurynome (an Oceanid) caught him and nursed him to health.

Poseidon and I both found Thetis a comely maiden, but we'd heard a prophesy that her eldest child by any god would raise hell in the upper echelons of our pantheon. To avoid this, we married her off to Peleus, a mortal. Their wedding was a legendary fiasco—it started the Trojan War! (See my **Eris** entry for details.) Eventually, Thetis and Peleus produced the great Greek hero, Achilles. In an attempt to bestow her young son with immortality, Thetis dipped him in the River Styx. Unfortunately, she neglected to submerge the heel by which she held the boy. That tragic mistake led to his downfall. I still get weepy thinking about it.

I wonder how Thetis is doing these days, now that Peleus has moved on? I hear she's living the peasant life somewhere in Argos. I was really fond of that Nymph—we had a couple nice moments, and I trusted her like no other god. She even fought by my side during the Pantopes coup a few years back! Somebody told me she had another kid after Achilles. I should drop in sometime.

Titans | *Elder but Stupid Gods*

The less we say about these fools, the better. These pre-Olympian gods ruled the cosmos under the leadership of my father, Kronos, who had defeated and overthrown his own father, Ouranos, the primordial god-king. But then my siblings and I made our own move and cast all the Titan gods (including Dad) into Tartaros after a lengthy yet oddly boring series of battles. The Olympians, as we are called, now rule the cosmos, and always will, I'm pretty sure. The only guy who gave me any serious trouble was this rumbling, clownish monster named Typhon. (See **Typhon** below.)

Typhon | *Four-Eyed Storm Giant*

Who is this guy, with his silly shoulder serpents? A while back, Typhon rose up out of nowhere and brazenly challenged my rule of the cosmos, vowing to free the Titans I'd just defeated. He called himself "Destroyer of Gods" and claimed to be born of Gaia herself! Look, I won't say he was a pushover—at first, my thunderbolts just bounced off his thick, ugly exoskeletal horn-head. And well . . . the guy did take me hostage and pulled out all my leg muscles. That was unpleasant.

But after a little supercharging . . . and a deep dive into my bag of power moves . . . I managed to cast him down into the sulfurous stink of Tartaros. Then I slammed Chryse's mountain right on top of him. Nice, eh? I sleep like a baby every night knowing that Typhon has been festering down there in anger for a thousand years and can never escape. Isn't it great how when bad things get buried down deep, you don't have to think about them anymore and never have to face them again?

◇ ◇ ◇

Wraiths | *Corrupted Mortal Heroes*

Brimming with despair, these dark entities are the shadows of fallen mortal heroes, risen from Tartaros and condemned to roam the earth seeking revenge! For what, I have no idea. All I know is they're angry. And I'm told they delegate a lot of their murderous tasks to minions called Shades (see **Shades**). Personally, I've never seen any of these foul things around Chryse. If you encounter one, please contact Security immediately.

Zeno of Citium | *Mortal Stoic Philosopher*

Born in Citium on Cyprus, southeast of Greece, this fellow was big on peace of mind, goodness, and a life of virtue. Zeno moved to Athens and founded Stoicism, a school of philosophy that put a lot of emphasis on being levelheaded, living in the moment, and just accepting what life brings, no matter how "good" or "bad" things seem to be. Zeno also posited that Nature is rational, and the universe is governed by reason. Hooo boy! This guy wouldn't have lasted two days in my court on Mount Olympos. Also, Zeno clearly never visited Tartaros. That place is insane—it literally makes no sense. However, I admit I'm fond of Zeno's famous quote: "It's better to trip with your feet than with your tongue." Now that's my kind of philosophy.

Zeus | *Greatest God Ever*

What can I say here? It's good to be king. What I say, goes. I steal a lot of wives, and I toast a lot of guys who displease me. Okay, I drink too much, but somehow things always work out.

◇ ◆ ◇

Nice work, Daidalos! Even Gaia was impressed. And you know how snobby she can be about landscaping issues.

King's Peak

The Forgelands

Grove of Kleos

Gates of Tartaros

War's Den

Valley of Eternal Spring

Clashing Rocks

Chryse: A Travel Guide

Ah, Chryse! Furrowed with freshwater streams and ocean inlets, our Golden Isle is a truly incredible paradise.

You like sun-dappled valleys? We've got 'em. Vertiginous buttes? I'm a huge fan of buttes, the bigger the better. What about mountainous shoulders cloaked in arboreal evergreen? Sure, we've got those too. (Full disclosure: I'm borrowing these ridiculous descriptions from Prometheus, our favorite tortured poet, who says travel guides are supposed to sound like this.)

The point is, as natural beauty goes, you really can't beat this place.

Deities of the smart set all vacation on the Golden Isle—though to be honest, even Koalemos shows up at our beach cookouts, and he's the God of Stupidity.

◇ ◇ ◇

The Layout

Chryse is actually a cluster of seven unique biomes—pretty amazing geographic variety, considering they border each other on just 27.5 square kilometers of real estate.

Not sure what the place originally looked like, but Daidalos clearly did some serious landform modifications. Some say he hired Gigantes Brothers for the heavy terrain work, then brought in Wood Nymph Lawn & Garden for the finer details. Whatever the case,

the guy did a heck of a job, I have to hand it to him.

As you tour the place, notice that Daidalos has designed each region to honor a patron god, adding a ginormous statue of each patron carved from a massive rock pillar. Each area is loaded with myth-based puzzles and challenges too.

So, hold on to your tram seats, folks. You won't see anything like Chryse, certainly not anywhere else on earth.

> ## WARNING! Please Do Not Feed the Wildlife!
> Chryse wildlife will extend any illicit feeding activity by extracting your entrails.

About Those Myth Challenges

Here on Chryse, Daidalos memorialized so many of our crazy stories. He did so in cleverly interactive ways, crafting thematic puzzles and other challenges based on some of the greatest tales ever told: Zeus Crushes Kronos, Zeus Turns Guy into Werewolf, Leda and the Swan (Zeus), Zeus Abducts Ganymede, Zeus Saves World from Stupid Kid in Sun Chariot, plus a bunch of stuff done by lesser gods and mortal so-called "heroes." Also, grisly monster legends.

What a hoot! Daidalos's myth challenges include navigation trials, constellation tests, musical listening

quizzes using lyres, fresco tile puzzles, and other tasks, including feats of archery worthy of Odysseus himself. Successful completion can earn rewards, but mostly you just feel super good about yourself. And isn't that what's really important?

Anyway, I'm glad you know your gods so well now. (You did check out my alphabetized roster, right?) Now we can take a much more informed tour of the island.

◇ ◆ ◇

A Note on the Island Locals

Visitors: Please ignore any mortals you see meandering about the island. These are resident staff—i.e., the people who maintain Chryse and live here year-round.

Our crack team includes:
- Dock & farm workers
- Transportation & delivery personnel —wagon drivers, etc.
- Division of Statue Polishers
- Security
- Forestry & Wildlife Management
  - Rangers
  - Animal feeders
  - Dung shovelers
- Landscaping Services
- Facility & Infrastructure Maintenance

  - Maintenance and repair of buildings, shrines, bridges, walkways & trails
  - Custodial services (janitors)
- Human Resources
  - Basically, one Cyclops named Lenny

Most staff are tolerable and unassuming, although I find it hard to fathom why they work so hard. I guess they're trying to "make a living." Or maybe my constant threats keep everyone on their toes, ha ha. To be perfectly honest, I'm constantly fighting the urge to turn the entire Fifth Age of Humanity into stone. Nothing personal, you understand. Let's just call it "creator's remorse."

In any case, don't talk to staff.

◇ ◆ ◇

Muse, sing of Hermes, the luck-bringing messenger
of the immortals. He consorts with all mortals and
immortals—little he profits, but through the dark
night, he continually tricks. —Homer

Clashing Rocks

·❧ Introduction ❧·

I suppose it's fitting that Chryse's main harbor and official Port of Entry is located in the region devoted to Hermes. After all, he is the God of Travelers. Island tourists probably feel good seeing his grinning face and that weird snaky caduceus looming over them. Ironically, Hermes is also god of thieving and trickery. Don't be shocked when your wallet disappears during the Grove of Kleos nature hike: *"Safe travels, folks! We appreciate the generous donation!"*

Also: I have to admit . . . a lot of Olympian stuff starts with Hermes. As Messenger of the Gods, everything flows through him. He plans all the good parties, lines up the band, the DJs. When we're starving for takeout, he takes everybody's orders, does pickup, it takes him like fifteen minutes. I mean, the guy wears winged shoes. Hermes is also the conduit for a lot of our corporate communications. So again, it certainly makes sense that you'd start your Golden Isle adventure by dropping anchor down south in Hermes Harbor.

Quick Overview

Topography

An ocean inlet separates Clashing Rocks from the rest of the Golden Isle. The place is aptly named—a rugged knot of rocky outcroppings, ringed by tall rock pillars hewn from ancient granite mesas. We're talking rocks piled on more rocks, with willowy dried grasses and a few trees layered on top. A *lot* of rocks, is what I'm saying. This little archipelago on the southern end of Chryse includes a protected harbor where visiting boats dock. Stone bridges connect its three main islets—the ones with primary structures. A fourth islet and a cluster of rock towers sprout from the water to the south.

Wildlife

Not a lot of wildlife in this small, isolated region—mostly blackbirds and wild boar, some feral chickens, maybe a bear or two. I've heard reports of the occasional Harpy harassing tourists, but this is rare—most Harpies are down in Tartaros screeching at Typhon, their deadbeat dad. Hermes also claims that a winged horse named Laurion gallops across the southernmost islet from time to time, and a terrifying triple-headed Chimera hangs out on one of the rock mesas. Sounds like mushroom-fueled myths to me!

Architecture and Design

The buildings on Clashing Rocks all feature classical design—symmetry, marble, lots of columns. Hey, you can't go wrong with a colonnade! The more Doric, the better, I always say. And since Hermes loves to bore everyone with his "Remember when I invented the lyre?" stories, Daidalos went nuts with the motif, lining the roofs of buildings and bridges with lyre casts. Yes, Hermes is one of our best musicians, I admit that. I just wish he'd stop hogging all the "Stairway to Heaven" solos and maybe convince his goatish kid Pan to take a shower once in a while.

⟨ South Cluster ⟩

Down at the southernmost end of Clashing Rocks, this ring of towering rock formations includes a larger islet with a pair of massive oak trees, some cozy huts for the local help, a cow statue (it's Io, I'm told), and one of Daidalos's insane archery puzzles. Shrines sit atop a couple of the other natural rock pillars; I've never checked them out myself, but I hear the guard details are brutal. Good swimmers can also explore water-level caves for hidden treasure.

Io, Hera, and Argus Panoptes

In my crazy youth—who am I kidding? I don't age!—I had a torrid affair with a mortal princess named Io. As always, Hera found out and took revenge on the girl, turning her into a white heifer.

That was bad enough, but then Hera assigned the hundred-eyed giant named Argus Panoptes, one of her loyal servants, to guard the cow girl. This big guy never slept! Or at least, he always had a few eyes open, looking in every compass direction.

So, I sent Hermes, master of music and spoken charms, to lull the big goon to slumber. My kid played the lyre, the panpipes, told boring stories. Finally, all the eyes closed, all one hundred of them, and Argus Panoptes started snoring like a sawmill. Then Hermes herded Io back to me. Oddly, hanging out with her was still hot. Who would have thought dairy farmer cosplay could be so much fun?

◇ ◇ ◇

⟨ Harbor Islet ⟩

This small island is where visitors arrive on Chryse. Protected from the elements and sea churn by the ring of South Cluster rocks, the beach dock here marks the starting point of your Golden Isle adventure. Some of the main attractions include:

Port of Entry

After your harrowing sea voyage from the mainland, you disembark at the southern beach. Climb the stone staircase into the main processing center, tucked up against a cliff. Inside, your boatload of fellow survivors is divided into tour groups and assigned guides—usually demigods trying to impress Aphrodite. Then you ascend the winding stairs up the cliff to access the island's main level. Be sure to tip the armed guard at the top! (He'll remember if you don't.)

Temple of Hermes

Directly up the path from the Port of Entry squats the temple devoted to Hermes. It's typical temple stuff, honoring this and worshipping that. The focal point of its west wing is the Hermes statue, winged helmet and all, outside a small music chamber. Across the lobby, the east wing houses a souvenir stand, some vending machines (courtesy of Hephaistos), and a few gender-neutral restrooms. Several paths from the main building lead to other shrines and outbuildings of the complex where you can make offerings to (or, in my case, make fun of) the Messenger of the Gods.

Messenger of the Gods: The Statue of Hermes

Hewn from a rock tower, this Hermes carving stands way too tall and wields his famous winged staff, the caduceus—it symbolizes his role as herald and messenger. It also represents commerce. And negotiating peace. And other stuff—it can be whatever you want, apparently, which is how ancient symbols work. The twin snakes entwined on it are said to represent all snakes, or maybe just two snakes, or possibly have nothing to do with snakes whatsoever, other than, you know, being snakes. I do happen to know that Apollo gave Hermes the caduceus in exchange for the sweet lyre Hermes invented. Seems like a fair trade.

Big Lyre Spring

This eyesore rises up behind a nice little freshwater spring that bubbles up and flows to a waterfall. The huge lyre is actually playable, which is great if you happen to be huge as well. Sorry, mortal tourists—I guess you could shoot arrows at its strings? A cobblestone path wends around the spring, great for contemplative strolls or birdwatching or souvenir rock hunting or any other mortal activity marking time until you die.

Hermes invented the lyre, of course, fashioning the first one from a tortoiseshell and sheep guts . . . which is pretty grisly when you think about it. The Hermes lyre symbol adorns the region's rooftops, and several lyre-related music puzzles can be found in Clashing Rocks. I'm told you can win Coins of Charon if you play the right notes. Good luck!

◇ ◇ ◇

Central Islet

A stone bridge runs from Harbor Islet to this largest islet of the Clashing Rocks group. Some interesting stuff here, including a big freaking rock shaped like a tortoise. Points of interest include:

Nike's Stadium

After you cross the bridge, you pass a Hermes shrine for offerings (the guy's always looking for handouts) to find a really impressive stadium featuring a racetrack. Could this be the famous venue where Hermes raced Apollo in the first Olympiad? Note the statue of Nike at the finish line, holding the victor's wreath. Man, that girl really loves hanging out with jocks.

> *The Great Race—Hermes vs. Apollo*
> *Hermes is famous for being swift of foot, but he's also infamously cocky by nature. When I convened the very first Olympic Games to celebrate my victory over Pop Kronos and the Titans, Hermes immediately challenged his half brother Apollo to a running race. I'm sure he figured it was an easy win, given that Apollo sits around all day writing verse, eating pastries, and taking script meetings with the Muses. But despite his blinding speed and winged heels, our golden-haired pretty boy got distracted and lost! Thus, Apollo won the very first laurel wreath.*

Caretaker's Village and Sheep Farm

Just past Nike's Stadium, the main walkway runs under a rock arch where a narrow path branches off to the right. This leads up onto a plateau where a lot of the Golden Isle foodservice staff live. Terraced hillsides, stone-fence enclosures, crops and pomegranate orchards, quaint brick huts and grain-filled silos . . . very picturesque, if you're into the pungent odor of animal dung. The locals grow their own food and raise livestock, including some really angry blue chickens. One family has an entire barnyard filled with sheep statues. Am I the only one who finds that disturbing?

> *Hermes, God of Shepherds*
> *Sure, he acts hip, but Hermes is actually a very pastoral fellow. Don't tell Aphrodite, but the guy loves sheep. I've seen him stagger around drunk for hours with a lamb on his shoulders. These locals with their sheep statues are clearly in the right god region.*

Temple of Midas

You can't miss this place. Take the right fork at the crossroads (marked by a creepy Herm of Hermes bust—a head on a square pillar) to find this impressive edifice dedicated to the great and foolish King Midas. Check out the front portico and all that gleaming gold finish work! Midas was pals with Hermes's son Pan, so Daidalos also dropped in a statue of the hircine kid on the waterfront just outside the main temple's northeast exit.

Midas and Pan

Everybody's heard of King Midas, right? After Dionysos granted him a wish, everything he touched turned into gold. But here's why the Temple of Midas is located in Clashing Rocks: Pan, son of Hermes, was a very close associate of Midas. In fact, Midas was a huge fan of Pan's music. Wore Pan T-shirts, followed his annual concert tour, hung out backstage with the Satyrs, etc.

I remember one of our big festivals—I think it was Zeuschella—Pan and Apollo were jamming onstage and got into a heated battle. Pan would huff out a reedy shriek; Apollo would answer with a molten lyre riff. The crowd went wild. But then somebody (okay, me) decided to make it a contest and appointed King Midas as judge—hey, I didn't know what a fanboy he was. When he picked Pan as best musician, an irritated Apollo gave the poor king donkey ears. I thought it was funny as hell.

The Pointing Snitch

Here's a fun myth challenge for you, folks! From the Temple of Midas, head northwest through another cluster of worker huts (again: please don't query the locals or I'll shrink you into salamander food) to find a statue of a pointing man. This is Battus, the guy who saw Hermes steal Apollo's prized herd of cattle. He's pointing across the waterfall to their "hiding place"—a cliffside cave that only opens if you can solve a three-switch puzzle! Inside, you can access an elaborate shrine with a treasure chest, a lyre music challenge, and a bunch of votive cows symbolic of Apollo's stolen herd. Don't fall off the cliffs trying to reach it! The Chryse Tourism Office does not offer refunds for death events.

Battus the Rat

Funny story. Hermes, who was very young but feeling his oats, stole Apollo's prized herd of fifty grass-fed Arkadian cattle. (Hermes made them walk backward to screw up the hoofprint tracking.) A shepherd named Battus witnessed the crime; after Hermes gave him a heifer, he promised not to snitch. But Hermes soon returned in disguise and offered Battus a nice reward for information leading to the stolen herd. When Battus pointed the way, Hermes instantly turned the rat into limestone. So . . . is this a statue of Battus? Or is it Battus himself, petrified? I'll have to ask my dear friend Daidalos. Oh, wait, I can't.

Tortoise Island

If you go left at the Herm of Hermes crossroads, you encounter the gargantuan figure of a tortoise sculpted from a rock mound in the middle of a lagoon. What a

beautiful creature! The views from atop its head and shell are pretty cool, if you have a knack for climbing. Apparently, you can also access a secret cave via a puzzle mechanism just under the tortoise's chin.

Hermes Invents the Lyre

The story goes that one day, Hermes wandered half-drunk outside his favorite god cave in Arkadia to find an ancient tortoise with an exquisite shell lumbering past. In typical godly fashion, he slaughtered the beautiful thing, scraped out its shell, and put notches on each end. Then he butchered a nearby sheep and stretched seven strands of its guts across the shell. The result of all this carnage was a divine musical instrument emitting tones so heavenly it could drown out even the Sirens' song.

Lair of the Minotaur

I've been told Daidalos designed this pillar-lined enclosure as a supermax detention facility in case any scary creature—like, say, another Minotaur—managed to make its way onto the island. Sitting on an isolated plateau surrounded by steep cliffs on one side and a sheer drop-off on the other, the compound certainly seems secure. Given his history back on Crete, I can understand how the inventor might be paranoid about monsters.

◇ ◇ ◇

⚡ Islet of Seers ⚡

Okay, folks, this is where Chryse really starts getting interesting. As you approach the stone bridge leading to the northwest island of the Clashing Rocks archipelago, the monumental Temple of Apollo looms ahead—magnificently, I must say. Before you cross, you might want to try the lyre music puzzle at the Hermes shrine just off the main road. Then head straight for the Oracle!

Temple of Apollo (Oracular Services)

I mean, just look at that gorgeous façade, people—an impressive six-column portico that looks like something right out of Apollo's personal sketchbook of happy dreams. Step inside the great main doors into the cavernous cella, and marvel at (but don't touch) the passage to the *adyton*, the restricted inner sanctum reserved for the Great Oracle. The Tourism Office tells me visitors can buy a personal prophecy session, but it will cost you an arm and a leg . . . possibly literally, depending on the Oracle's mood.

Winds of Aiolos

Somewhere in the vicinity of Apollo's oracle, our half-witted God of Wind stashes his breezy goods in jars. I know times are still ancient around here, but come on, jars? I hear he tried to make a peanut butter sandwich last week and accidentally unleashed a small typhoon on the West Indies.

Votive Shrine to Hermes

When you head upstairs past the Temple of Apollo and cross the footbridge, be sure to make a votive offering at the Hermes shrine on the left. Bronze animal statuettes are nice. Cash is better. Adventurers might want to check out the water tunnel behind the shrine. It leads to a stunning vista, with the fabulous Hall of the Gods silhouetted on a distant plateau.

The Observatory Complex

In honor of Hermes's obsession with the stars, Daidalos constructed a truly impressive astronomy center dedicated to the exalted study of the sky and heavenly bodies—two topics about which I know a lot, believe me. For example, at the top of the stairs you'll find one of the architect's fiendish myth challenges, where hapless tourists try to gather glowing orbs to form the star pattern of the Lyra constellation.

Success at the constellation puzzle gives you access to the feathers of Daidalos's infamous wings, about as useless a reward as I can imagine. As the plaque reads: "Welcome to the Golden Isle—in remembrance of my greatest success and greatest failure. May the gods accept my offering, and may I see you again, Ikaros." Sad, isn't it? He never did see his boy again, the poor *dear*.

Lyra—the Dulcet Lyre of Hermes, Apollo, and Orpheus

I mentioned earlier how Hermes crafted the first lyre from tortoiseshell and strands of sheep gut. That legendary lyre, called Lyra, had quite a history. First off, Hermes gave it to Apollo to atone for rustling a herd of his cattle. Apollo loved the lyre's soothing tones so much that he let Hermes keep the stolen cows, and even threw in a set of steak knives.

Later, Apollo hosted a cookout (Hermes provided the beef, of course) and heard his pal Orpheus strumming the lyre with such soulful beauty that Apollo immediately gifted it to his friend. Orpheus used the instrument to successfully woo the Nymph Eurydice. But after a venomous snake killed the poor girl, Orpheus made the perilous journey to the Underworld to plead for her return. His Lyra tuneage so charmed Hades that the Underworld king agreed to let Eurydice leave . . . as long as Orpheus didn't look back on the way out. Which of course he did. Oops! Eurydice got sucked back into eternal shade. Orpheus pleaded for a second chance, but Hades has a strict no-return policy. "What, you think we're Costco?" he said.

Orpheus spent the rest of his life as a wandering poet and minstrel, mourning his lost love. Man, the guy could charm anything with his musical skills, even rocks and scorpions and whatnot. That Lyra was so remarkable that I called an executive god meeting and we agreed to place it in the sky eternally as the Lyra constellation.

Rooftop Orrery

One other attraction is worth a closer look in the complex. Atop the circular observatory building, Daidalos and his Kamikos engineers constructed a truly resplendent rooftop mechanical device called an orrery. This clockwork-style mechanical assembly is a type of planetarium, modeling the movements of heavenly orbs. Amusingly, its very existence suggests the orbs move according to the dictates of physical laws . . . when everybody knows the Ruler of the Sky makes all the magic happen!

Hermes, Creator of Astronomy? Really?

Hermes likes to tell me "the stars tell stories"— okay, fine, whatever—and claims to have created the science of astronomy. This is disputed by important experts (i.e., me). I certainly admit the kid took an early interest in the constellations— you know, those big starry clusters that I happen to rule? Yeah, I'm Ruler of the Sky. I'm also the king of all gods. Sometimes Hermes forgets this little fact.

◇ ◇ ◇

Muse, tell me the deeds of golden Aphrodite,
who subdues mortal men and birds in air,
and the creatures on land and sea. Grant me
a song! Stir up my sweetest passions.
—Homer

Valley of Eternal Spring

Introduction

When Daidalos tackled the challenge of sculpting a playground worthy of the Goddess of Love, well . . . I guess it's not surprising that Aphrodite's region ended up with the most voluptuous assets on Chryse. What a property! Just across a narrow band of sea from Clashing Rocks, the Valley of Eternal Spring sprawls over rolling emerald countryside so lush it's hard to believe the two regions are neighbors. Up north, spectacular water terraces and lakes surround a massive tree known as Gaia's Soul. Then the valley waters descend down a network of rivulets and streams flowing west and south to the sea.

Like Aphrodite herself, the land is ridiculously luxuriant and fruitful. So, naturally, she loves every nook and cranny of it. The place exudes fertility, right? Look, this woman has driven gods and mortals alike completely crazy with desire. She's so hot she starts wars! I had to marry her off to my boring misanthropic son Hephaistos just to get her off the market. I know that's not very woke, but guys were pulling some really lunatic stunts to get her attention. And yeah, I've heard the whisper campaign about "Zeus the control freak." I don't care what anybody says—I did it for her own good.

I will say this: the only thing more striking than Aphrodite's beauty is her wickedly acerbic wit. In a less alluring package, it would be distasteful, maybe even ugly. With her, it just makes you want to be bad too. Very, very bad. It sure would be a shame if Aphy ever lost her quintessence of snark.

◇ ◇ ◇

Topography

Aphrodite's region is a dazzling patchwork of river valleys, meadowlands, groves, lakes, and (fittingly) a lot of erupting rock pillars, ha! A big ocean bay arcs inland from the west, essentially splitting the region in two. The bay is the final receptacle of rivers wending around the great soaring statue of Aphrodite, the center point of the region. Look for wooded glens with pomegranate and golden apple trees as well as pink laurel orchards. Wild gardens and flower-dotted meadowlands offer bright bursts of color to lucky visitors. To the far north, traverse a glistening blue waterscape of terraced pools, and yes, this *entire* paragraph was dictated to me by Prometheus.

Wildlife

The Valley of Eternal Spring offers home and sustenance to a substantial population of wild animals. Birds of all kinds feast on the orchard fruits, while bears, feral boars, and regal stag herds roam the region. You might also find an occasional wild horse or two. And lots of insects. Billions of them. Buzzy little bastards. None of them dare bite gods, but the cacophony at night is so maddening you want to rip out your immortal hair.

Architecture and Design

Daidalos wisely relied on the Tholos architectural style when designing the major structures in Aphrodite's region. Everybody knows she loves big round things with domes on top. The Hall of the Gods and the two regional palaces are classic examples, featuring rings of columns supporting circular domes and covered with decorative growth, plus numerous circular plazas and pools. Round, open, bucolic, sexy—perfect for the Goddess of Love! The master architect also went with a clamshell glyph motif when lining the rooftops of key buildings, in honor of Aphrodite's foamy ocean birth.

◇ ◇ ◇

⟫ South Coast ⟪

The terrain directly across the inlet from Clashing Rocks is gorgeous if largely undeveloped wilderness. Steep headlands rise from the sea but angle downward as you head southwest, eventually dropping to sea level to form a shoreline of beaches, low bluffs, and river deltas. The western end of this coastal stretch is more developed, featuring statuary and a number of myth challenges primarily devoted to Eros—God of Love and Aphrodite's pampered son—as well as to the legendary trials of his lovely spouse Psykhe.

Wedding Cave of Tethys and Oceanos

As you tour the coastline, keep an eye out for a set of giant clamshells in the river estuary fed by a cascading trio of waterfalls. Follow the river upstream to find a cave nestled between two of the waterfalls. This is the very place where we celebrated the blessed union of Tethys and Oceanos, god of the mighty river that encircles the world. What a ceremony that was! Be sure to snap a selfie in front of the statues depicting one of their infamous connubial "discussions." (We could hear their fights for miles around.)

Once you see the happy couple, you might want to meet the family. Follow the fish! Matching sets of shark statues lead off the beach and out to two golden pillars in the water. These mark the location of an underwater platform guarded by two great statues of Hera's favorite animal, the lion. Anyone who can perform a surface dive and hold their breath can flip the switch there. This reveals a shrine to Hera, everybody's favorite peacemaker, back at the river mouth!

Here, visitors might think the Hall of the Gods, looming so majestically just to the north, is the next tour destination. But guess what? The Hall of the Gods is for gods. You're not a god. So, you're not permitted in our hall. Seriously, mortal trespassers will be smote. You're not welcome here.

Oceans of Offspring!

Tethys and Oceanos had what you might call a spicy relationship. In the first years after their wedding, they spent approximately 94.3 percent of their waking hours engaged in activity that produced three thousand daughters—the sea Nymphs called the Oceanids—and three thousand sons, the river gods known as the Potamoi. Good god, no wonder Oceanos is walking bowlegged these days.

All that baby making was fun, I'm sure, but having six thousand kids running around puts a lot of child-rearing stress on a marriage. (Not that I would know. If Hera and I didn't like a kid we just tossed it off the mountain.) The hyperfertile couple often bickered. I mean, Tethys was a Titan, for god's sake. She could be a real monster. And Oceanos was so passive aggressive, always ebbing and flowing, ebbing and flowing. A guy like that could drive any wife to homicidal rage.

Hera the Marital Therapist?

My dear wife Hera was quite a handful as a child, and our mother, Rhea, already had her hands full dealing with our psychopath dad, Kronos. So, she handed Hera over to Tethys and Oceanos for raising—because, you know, they had a bit of experience with that task. Hera truly loved her foster parents. And they loved her so much in return she became a trusted mediator, helping them resolve their frequent and frightening marital rows. Ironic isn't it, that Hera could be such an effective peacekeeper in any marriage but her own?

The Trials of Psykhe

Instead, I recommend you continue along the coastal trail. This route leads through a region designed to showcase Aphrodite's squirrely son Eros, God of Obsessive Love, and his obsessive love for the supermodel Psykhe. The road meanders past several different myth challenges related to their forbidden love.

The first exhibit you reach is Eros the Archer. Note how he's aiming at Psykhe, just up the hill? She's on the cliff, gazing at the ocean, unaware that some sneaky little god boy is trying to impale her with an arrow. Ah, love! This spot also includes a tough archery-related myth challenge that I can't imagine any mortal visitor successfully completing, ever. (In it, Eros shoots an arrow that ends up igniting his own torch of love!)

A bit further down the path you find a devilishly difficult fresco puzzle depicting Psykhe and . . . yeah, that's a bunch of ants. (Don't ask.) Beyond that, a path fork to the right leads to a pair of impossible navigation challenges designed for somebody with superhuman agility and maybe a paraglider. One commemorates Psykhe's golden sheep trial; the other marks her effort to scoop dark Underworld water. Nike waits at the end of each course, waving a laurel wreath as a tease. My advice: Don't even try them. You'll fail and likely be maimed.

Eros and Psykhe

Aphrodite really hated other attractive women, whether goddess, Nymph, or mortal—especially mortal. When she beheld Psykhe, legendary beauty, she was so jealous that she sent her kid Eros to stalk the poor girl. His orders: nail Psykhe with a love arrow the moment she got near any disgusting, vile beast so she'd fall in love with it. But as Eros snuck up on Psykhe he accidentally nicked himself with his own arrow . . . and went nuts for the girl! (Although frankly, she was so hot the arrow nick was probably irrelevant.)

After some initial drama, the two really hit it off. But Eros knew his mom would be livid, so he kept the relationship secret. Both lovers knew they'd have to gain Aphrodite's blessing eventually.

Aphrodite's Nasty Trials

So, Psykhe and Eros fell in love. It was nice at first. But eventually, all the sneaking around got old. Psykhe decided to prove herself to Eros's mom, Aphrodite. Did the goddess ask her to kill Hydras or catch three-headed dog monsters? No, she made Psykhe sort seeds, snag sheep wool, fill a water flask, and then beg Persephone for some makeup. I'm not kidding. Those were the trials.

But goofy as they sound, it was no cakewalk:

Psykhe's first trial—sorting a massive mound of mixed barley, chickpea, beans, and lentils into separated piles in a short time limit—would have been totally impossible except for help from a friendly column of ants. That's right. Friendly ants. Something I've never seen in my countless years of all-seeing, so please count me as skeptical.

The second trial—to retrieve a tuft of wool from a herd of (get this) "fierce man-eating sheep" —still makes me chuckle, although it turns out

these rams were indeed quite fearsome, with sharp horns and poisonous teeth. Their wool was actually pure gold, and people were always trying to steal it. But Psykhe waited until they got sleepy in the sun, then slipped in close for a quick clipping. Two trials down, two to go!

Next Aphrodite demanded that Psykhe collect a flask of black water from an icy waterfall that dropped down terrifying cliffs into the Underworld only to bubble back up into a surface spring. But a nice eagle passing by agreed to help her . . . and come on now, really? Friendly ants, nice eagles? What is this, a Disney movie?

Anyway, it all came down to the fourth and final trial: Aphrodite ordered Psykhe to visit Persephone, queen of the Underworld, and ask her for a basket of . . . I kid you not . . . cosmetics. Aphrodite's own beauty ointment, to be exact. Infiltrating "Hades Land" is no easy task for a mere mortal, of course, but Psykhe showed spunk —she got across the Styx, snuck past hellish guards, dodged killer hounds, and scored the face lotion from Persephone. The queen told her not to look at it, but of course Psykhe couldn't resist. She peeked into the basket and some Hades smoke planted inside knocked her out! Eros had to come rescue her from eternal sleep.

In the end, I was so impressed by Psykhe's overall performance that I gave her a sip of ambrosia, making her immortal too. Eventually, even Aphrodite agreed that the girl proved her mettle and was a good match for her foppish son.

Eros's Haven

After you fail miserably at the myth challenges, slink across the bridges onto the southwest island to explore Eros's Haven, a snazzy wedding palace built for Eros and Psykhe. Aphrodite is quite fond of her son Eros, and Daidalos clearly reflected this love in his design. (To be honest, it's as much an homage to Aphrodite as it is to her loopy kid.) What a place for a happy ending!

Here you find a tricky constellation puzzle—can you arrange orbs into the Pisces constellation? Daidalos designed this one in honor of mother and son, celebrating their fishy escape from that idiot Typhon just before I kicked his storm-giant ass into Tartaros. Also under the Haven: in a dark sea-level cave far, far beneath the palace grounds (a good symbolic location) you can find a fresco puzzle depicting Psykhe's amusing meeting with Persephone in the Underworld.

Pisces: Escaping Typhon

Ever wonder why there are two fish in the Pisces constellation? Well, after I led my Olympian god squad to the brink of a glorious victory over the Titans, the grim losers had Gaia conjure up a mammoth monster named Typhon in a pathetic last-gasp effort to turn the tide against us. The big goon ran amok for a while, harassing any god he could find. At one point he had Aphrodite and her son, Eros, trapped on a seashore. As Typhon gloated and howled like a preening idiot, a school of bluefish swam up and invited Aphrodite to escape with them. She sneakily transformed both herself and Eros into fish, mingled with the school, and swam away. Typhon was so angry he stomped the water, sending a tsunami across the Aegean Sea. Later, in gratitude, Aphrodite put a pair of fish into the sky as the constellation Pisces.

Siren Island

Before you head into the Central Valleys, take a quick tour of this tiny bay island just northwest of Eros's Haven. See all the shipwrecks on its shore? Those poor mariners were lured by the enchanted music of the Sirens. Such voices! I can tell you, there are a lot of things I'd do to hear them. Be sure to light their torches to activate the switches that open the Siren's Temple. Inside, you'll find nice treasure and can listen to the small lyre's melody for replay on the region's Big Lyre, thus solving another myth challenge.

Siren Song

Everybody knows about the Sirens, right? These winged beauties own a nice island property with a sweet recording studio. If passing ships sail too close, the girls crank up their volume a bit. The sound is irresistible . . . literally. (Not really fair to other musicians—Sirens sweep the Grammys every year.) Any helmsman who hears a Siren's song is gripped with delirium and steers his ship directly into the rocky shoreline. As a result, Sirens accumulate a lot of good boat parts and other merchandise washing up on their beaches. I hear they make a killing in the resale market.

 Central Valleys

This large central stretch of the valley is dominated by two magisterial high points, the Hall of the Gods and the great statue of Aphrodite. As for other points of interest here . . . well, Aphrodite really loves lovely men. So Daidalos designed memorials to three of the loveliest ever—Adonis, Narcissus, and Endymion.

Shrine of Adonis

Directly across the river from all those "Trials of Psykhe" challenges (mentioned earlier in the South Coast section), a field of red roses undulates in front of a stately, pillar-lined shrine. Inside the shrine, the smooth alabaster face of Adonis, prettiest of go-go boys, gazes down on you. Enjoy the view, but don't step out of the tour wagon! The very boar that slayed Adonis (cleverly named "the Slayer of Adonis") guards the shrine, and quite jealously I might add—as jealous as Ares, it seems. Hmmm. Well, until somebody can dispatch the beast, you won't find it easy to reach the splendid fresco puzzle depicting the legendary goring event. Somebody really needs to give Security a buzz.

Note: if you follow the road up from the Adonis shrine, you'll find a village inhabited by attendants for the annual Festival of Adonia held in a nearby temple built into a rocky ravine. (Note Aphrodite's signature clamshells lining its roof.) The village includes local farmers who produce cabbages for the horribly smelly event. If it seems like a lot of cabbages are lying around, just remember that the whole thing is Aphrodite's idea and I'm not exactly privy to her thinking here.

Adonis and the Boar

Aphrodite was out for a woodland stroll one day when she discovered the mortal infant Adonis, swaddled in a box under a tree. Our favorite goddess of love wasn't big on childrearing (look how Eros turned out, always shooting people) so she handed off the kid to her Aunt Persephone down in the Underworld. But in an amusing twist, Adonis grew up to be an impossibly handsome young man. When Aphrodite saw him years later, she basically swooned. They started dating, she always picked up the tab, etc.

But dark Persephone has a nasty possessive streak, and she wouldn't give up Adonis. It turned into a real tug of war. The poor kid was always coming and going (and vice versa), so I had to step in and work out an equitable time-share arrangement. Unfortunately, during one handoff, Adonis ran into a wild boar the size of a Winnebago and was gored to death. What a shame. Who could have foreseen such a thing?

Note: Aphrodite had many jealous lovers. Some say Ares had something to do with the hoggish Slayer of Adonis. He wasn't keen on sharing Aphrodite with a mortal, especially one with such a big, uh . . . codpiece. Whatever. Look, it was all

for the best, okay? Aphy would have chewed up the kid and spit him out eventually. Adonis was not worthy of her.

Red Roses, Anemones, and Cabbages

Prometheus tells me that when Adonis was slain by the boar, Aphrodite fell upon him and shed such a flood of tears that they washed her gored lover's blood across the rosebush meadow, turning the flowers red! Not only that, but when she poured nectar on her lightweight consort's wounds, it dribbled into the fields and a new flower sprouted, the anemone, symbol of new life. Which sounds about as plausible as any other myth you hear around here, so . . . okay, I'll buy it.

But then the grieving Goddess of Love started the Festival of Adonia in honor of her slain boy toy. Every year, women across the land, mortal and goddess, princess and prostitute, all sob from the rooftops, mourning Aphrodite's loss. Every. Year. *They sing and dance and party hard, whirling around and howling about the freedom to choose who they get to ravish, I guess. And somehow, cooked cabbage became part of this godforsaken ritual. It smells like a sulfur mine for days around here.*

Narcissus Lily Pond

Now follow the road due north from all the Adonis crap, bearing toward the huge Aphrodite regional statue in the distance. Is this countryside idyllic or what? Take the right fork at the herm pillar and work your way down to a hidden spring-fed lily pond, dotted with water lilies and nestled in a watery canyon. (It sits just east of the Aphrodite statue.)

Here, a big statue of the famous self-lover Narcissus reclines on a small island, gazing deeply and lovingly down at the fresco puzzle nearby in the pond. Enter the shrine on the cliff face to unlock the fresco, and check out

the white sprays of narcissus in the cave chamber beyond. When solved, the fresco puzzle depicts the reflection of the self-absorbed lad in the water.

For the Love of Narcissus

Mortal son of Cephissus (a name I can't say without spraying spittle on my tunic), this young Boeotian hunter was exquisitely fetching but oblivious to love, leaving a string of broken hearts in his wake. One day Narcissus was tracking game and came upon a still pond. He crept up to find the most flawlessly gorgeous creature he'd ever seen. Yes, it was his own reflection. Absolutely captivated by the beauty gazing up at him from the water, Narcissus was paralyzed by unrequited love and could only stare back, unable to move. As a result, he starved to death. After a while, all that was left of his lovely corpse was the narcissus flower that bears his name today.

Temple of the Moon Goddess/Cave of Endymion

From the Narcissus pool, head east across the river into a rugged badlands of stacked granite mesas. Keep climbing until you find a high plateau with golden pillars marked with glowing blue moon glyphs. This is the Temple of the Moon Goddess. If you can manage to push the big moon-shaped boulder uphill to its switch pad, it unlocks a navigation myth challenge. (Don't tell Sisyphos you pushed a boulder all the way up onto a hilltop and it stayed in place! He's depressed enough as it is.)

When the horn sounds, navigate the course to the finish beacon at the Nike statue. Then check out the cave full of sleeping cushions behind her. This is a replica of the grotto where I put the mortal shepherd-prince Endymion into a permanent snooze for the moon goddess, Selene. She wanted to watch him sleep forever and do god knows what to the kid.

◇ ◇ ◇

Endymion and the Moon Goddess

The young Aiolian shepherd Endymion was yet another one of those implausibly good-looking mortal boys, like Adonis and Narcissus, whose good looks drove goddesses to fixate on them in unhealthy ways. One day, Endymion snuck into a cave on Mount Latmus for a quick nap. As he snored away, the loony Titan moon goddess Selene wandered in and immediately fell in love with the snoring hunk. She was so smitten by Endymion's sleeping countenance (and other parts south, no doubt) that she begged me to zap him with a perpetual sleep spell. Selene has a real dark side and can be kind of scary, so I didn't argue, I just granted her wish.

No big deal, right? Except, as it turns out, Selene didn't just "watch him sleep." Poor Endymion fathered fifty daughters by her without ever waking! I can only imagine what his dreams were like. If the guy ever regains consciousness, I expect we'll see some sort of legal proceeding regarding consent issues, not to mention all the child support payments. Hmmm, I'll have to let Athena handle that.

Lion's Mesa

Find the high mesa on the neck of land extending from the farthest eastern edge of the valley. Almost impossible to reach, this little plateau once served as home to the legendary Nemean Lion. The Tourism Board suggests you observe the big cat's lair from the next mesa over, in case other lions are about. Seriously: don't go up there unless you have a lot of cat treats.

The Nemean Lion

This terrifying cat-spawn of Typhon was a real favorite of my dear wife, Hera, who loves lions and hates most mortals. She deployed the beast into the wooded hills of Nemea near Argos to plague the nice people there for something or other they did or didn't do or maybe it was their annoying accent, doesn't really matter. We're gods, we make our own rules. Anyway, that explains its name, the Nemean Lion. The thing had a real craving for human flesh. It got pretty grisly around that countryside. Hera and I spent a number of evenings sipping glasses of ouzo, watching the action from our balcony.

Later, when King Eurystheus was gifted the servitude of Herakles, he immediately assigned the task of slaying the beast. One problem, though: the Nemean Lion had impenetrable golden fur that repelled even the sharpest of weapons, and its claws could slice through any armor. Because Herakles couldn't stab the big cat, he snuck into its cave and strangled it instead. Then, thanks to a clever tip from Athena, he used the creature's own claws to skin it. Herakles wore the skin frequently, since it made him essentially invincible to weapon attacks. He also thought it flattered his figure. Boy, was he wrong about that.

Goddess of Love: The Statue of Aphrodite

A nice way to conclude your tour of the Central Valleys district is to take in the spectacular 360-degree vistas from the towering regional statue of Aphrodite. It's actually an entire island, carved from the granite steps of a vertical bluff. Note how Aphrodite holds out an apple in her hand by way of welcome. Or is it a warning? Hard to know with that gal. Whatever the case, it depicts the Apple of Discord she won in that damned beauty contest—you know, the one that triggered the Trojan War. I must say, though, the views from atop that apple are breathtaking.

The Apple of Discord

Every tourist knows the gist of this story because all the Trojan War stuff is such a crux of Greek culture. But look, people, I was actually there. In fact, I was in charge, and I made the executive decision that got the apple rolling, so to speak, for better or worse. Here's what went down.

When King Peleus of Pythia (say that rapidly ten times) and the Nymph Thetis got married, I hosted a celebratory banquet. I left Eris off the invitation list even though literally everybody else was invited, because who wants the Goddess of Chaos knocking back mojitos at your party? Nobody, that's who. But then, as revenge for this snub, Eris engraved the words "To the Fairest" on a golden apple and tossed it into the hall like an incendiary device. Hera, Athena, and Aphrodite started fighting over it, each thinking it was obviously meant for her. What a catfight that was.

My solution was to appoint Paris, this vapid Trojan kid, to award the apple prize. I figured the rest of us would just laugh it off, since it would be the judgment of such a vacuous lightweight. Big mistake . . . and I'm god enough to admit it now. Aphrodite bribed Paris by offering him the love of Helen of Sparta, hottest mortal girl on the Peloponnesian Peninsula. Boom! Just like that, he hands Aphy the apple! (Hera had offered him the throne of Asia Minor plus untold riches, while Athena proffered eternal glory and renown in war —no contest, right?)

Folks, your Golden Isle tour will explore this tale further, including how it all played out, when you reach Aphrodite's palace. But for now, know that one stupid apple led to one of the bloodiest wars in human history, a ten-year affair that ended in the utter destruction of a perfectly lovely Mediterranean city-state.

Hall of the Gods

I saved the hall for last in this district because you can't go there, so why dangle its majesty in front of you like a blindingly brilliant gem? This is a place where only gods—plus certain mortal heroes blessed by gods—can come to hang out, have a few cocktails, consult, arrange trysts, nap, and retool. By "retool," I mean upgrade and customize gear and potions, or sharpen skills and godly powers. We also debate politics and check out the latest sports scores.

Some of the amenities up here include:

- **Bench of Zeus.** It's a rare god (and no mortal) who can handle my lightning. But if you can gather a few bolts, just trade them in here to boost your stamina.

- **Kylix of Athena.** Mortals can't really ingest ambrosia without suffering major gastrointestinal distress, but heroes can trade it in at this kylix for extended health benefits.

- **River Styx Cistern.** Here you can spend any rare Coins of Charon you've collected to boost your skills and godly powers.

- **Forge of Hephaistos.** Son Heph is happy (I think —I can never really read him) to let you spend adamantine shards to buff up your gear here!

- **Cauldron of Circe.** We gods use ingredients like mushrooms, figs, flower nectar, pomegranates, and golden amber to craft potions that enhance our divine powers. We can't let you tourists try this, due to liability issues.

- **Aphrodite's Beauty Chair.** This lets you change your looks in unbelievably fundamental ways—fun!

- **Hermes's Heroic Tasks Board.** Hermes keeps a list of tasks that gods and heroes can complete to win prizes and, even better, increase the number of fans who worship us on social media!

After you cross the wide river from the great Aphrodite statue, our Golden Isle tour takes you up verdant valleys carved by waterways and dotted with smaller shrines and temples. The most prominent features are a jumble of flat-topped granite pillars to the east; the spectacular sky-blue steps of the water terraces rising to the north; and of course, the region's other central landmark, the immense tree known as Gaia's Soul.

Big Lyre

Every region of the Golden Isle has a gigantic lyre on which to play the notes you hear at the various small lyre music challenges. Here's the big lyre for the Valley of Eternal Spring, just across the river north of the great Aphrodite statue.

Gaia's Soul

Easily one of Chryse's most striking features, this colossal tree rises like a billowing green thunderhead in the center of the Northern Waterways district. Gaia's Soul is so big it has its own weather patterns—a crazy network of strong updrafts that blow skyward around its trunk! Stretching up to the very heavens, the great tree is alive with birds, day and night. It really is the biggest living thing I've ever seen, except for possibly Typhon, although I wasn't really seeing straight when I punched his mammoth mouth.

The Necklace of Harmonia

From Gaia's Soul, the standard tour heads east across a bridge spanning the deep river gorge. Look for a plaza with a tall, beautiful statue of Aphrodite clad in golden robes. Behind her rises a golden domed pavilion with a *really* big necklace on the ground, wrapped around the structure. Another crazy Daidalos puzzle! But here's the really crazy thing: This one is based on an event that, according to my sources, hasn't even happened yet. I'm going to assume that Daidalos consulted with an Oracle of Delphi before whipping up this little design.

The necklace includes a massive medallion, but the inset amethyst is missing. The puzzle solution demands that you find all three broken pieces of the purple jewel and reassemble them in the setting. Tip: I wouldn't complete the task without a AAA-quality warrior in your tour group. Turns out the necklace is cursed—when repaired, the jewel summons a nasty Cyclops

hungering for mortal meat. A victory (however unlikely) over this monster unlocks a very difficult navigation challenge too.

The Cursed Wedding Gift

I had to consult the Oracles on this one, because apparently it involves some future shenanigans. For years, Aphrodite has cheated on her husband, my son Hephaistos, with my other son, Ares. What can I say? The acorn doesn't fall far from the tree. The illicit tryst has produced a truly lovely immortal child named Harmonia. Great kid. Big hearted. Happy. She's the Goddess of Harmony and Concord, for god's sake! She knits sweaters for everybody and takes in stray dogs. She bakes cupcakes for sad people.

But Hephaistos does not take any consolation from Harmonia's fundamental decency and sunny disposition. I hear he's vowed revenge for the infidelity . . . and true to his mother's creed, he's targeting not the perpetrators, but their innocent spawn. Slaving in his workshop for weeks, Heph has fashioned a future "wedding gift" for Harmonia—an exquisite necklace, gold and amethyst, but secretly imbued with a curse destined to bring woe and misfortune to any who possess it. I'm also told this so-called "Necklace of Harmonia" will pass down through generations of her family, with each new owner afflicted by some malady or misfortune even more horrible than the last.

Water Terraces

This remarkable waterscape of shimmering blue pools drops down from the north in an intricate arrangement of scalloped, overlapping terraces. It may be the most amazing landscaping job ever—quite a compliment from a guy who's been around a few millennia, right?

Sanctuary of the Lemnian Supplicants

As you work your way north up the watery steps, you'll start to notice a pungent odor wafting in the breeze. Mask up, tourists! Seriously, not kidding, wrap a thick bandana across your face. (If you don't have one, your tour guide will provide nose plugs.) Even with your nose covered, you smell it, right? That's the fetid scent of the infamous Lemnian women. After Aphrodite smote them with a smell so ghastly their male villagers wouldn't touch them, the women of Lemnos turned to the goddess in desperate supplication. She graciously gave them "sanctuary." Now they all work for pennies as attendants in her temple on the water terraces. Nice way to get cheap labor.

Curse of the Lemnian Women

I like to summer on Lesbos—really love those gals—and recently I heard a very interesting counter-narrative floating around that island. The canonical story is that one year the women of Lemnos got so involved in local gossip that they forgot to make their annual offering of cakes, salted bread, and honey to Aphrodite. So the love goddess, vindictive as always, cursed the poor gals with an odor so ghastly the men of Lemnos wouldn't come near them, let alone touch them.

Yeah, so that's the official story. But according to my Lesbos sources, what really happened is that the Lemnian women got tired of all the abuse and mansplaining from their husbands and slew the men in their sleep one night. Then they concocted the cover story, blaming everything on Aphrodite. The problem with that theory is that,

damn, those women really do smell bad. Hard to believe they befouled themselves just to have an alibi. To be perfectly honest, the odor is so horrifyingly putrid I've considered turning them all to stone just to put them out of their misery . . . but I'm pretty sure the stink would survive even petrification.

Lemnian men even had the gall to use the bad-smell story in order to justify cheating on their wives with women from Thrace. When the Lemnian women found out (and they always find out, don't they, guys?), they killed their husbands and set up a feminist commune. Later, the Argonauts wandered into this commune and slept with the women, so that makes the bad-smell angle seem kind of fishy, doesn't it? Also, after that, men across Greece started telling the "stinky curse" story to discourage their own wives from getting all feminist, dispatching them, and sleeping with Argonauts.

Admittedly, gender politics is a topic that we gods don't quite grasp. Maybe I'll get Athena to schedule a seminar?

◇ ◆ ◇

·} Western Cape {·

The western part of the Valley extends in a bulbous, river-split cape out into the ocean. Here tourists can find some of Daidalos's cleverest exhibits and shrines to Aphrodite, as well as the truly remarkable palace he built to honor the goddess.

Aphrodite's Pearl

Way up in the furthest northeast corner of the Valley of Eternal Spring, look for a deep cleft carved into the rugged badland mesas. At the head of this box canyon you can find a cluster of giant clamshells. In the largest one, Daidalos has placed a gigantic pearl, re-creating the one that Ouranos once tossed into the ocean. From the foam churned up by that legendary splash emerged Aphrodite, fully grown and, yes, pretty as a pearl! The Tourism Board tells me you can actually roll this huge replica all the way down the long narrow canyon to the sea . . . if you're strong enough.

Birth of Aphrodite

Oh, this is one of my favorites. Mom used to tell it all the time! Prometheus says it's a gruesome tale,

but what a drama queen he is—there's nothing unpleasant about it whatsoever. The story begins with a titanic battle between Kronos and Ouranos! You see, Dad was trying to overthrow Grandpappy and claim rulership of the cosmos. The battle was so fierce that it tore the earth from the heavens. (Our family squabbles are pretty epic.) The resultant earthquake was so powerful it jarred a huge pearl loose from its giant oyster, spitting it from the sea onto the shore.

But as the pearl flew past, Grandpappy Ouranos managed to snag it and, with a mighty heave, whipped it right back out into the ocean. The lustrous orb hit the water so hard that a frothy foam exploded to the surface. From that magical foam, the Goddess of Love rose like a fountain of unspeakable beauty. She stepped ashore, naked and fully grown, and reportedly said, "Hi, boys. Where can a lonely girl find a good cup of coffee in this town?"

◇ ◆ ◇

Meteora Village

Ready for a climb? Get ready to explore an exhibit depicting one of the really great Zeus tales. I love this one! Up in the northwest nook of the Western Cape, spot the totally shattered village sitting precariously atop a massive rock mesa called "the Meteora." (It's a brutal climb, but you paid for a AAA tour, so stop complaining.) This is the peaceful little hamlet that Hermes and I totally annihilated to teach the paranoid mortal bastards who lived there a lesson. God, that was fun!

And that's not all! After you explore the depressing ruins a bit, knocking down pillars if you can (ha ha, just kidding, you can't), head back down the Meteora and take a few steps west to find a small compound—a sweet little temple dedicated to yours truly, sitting next to a humble caretaker's cottage. This was the home of Baukis and Philemon; I rebuilt it after we absolutely crushed their village. I let them tend to my temple instead of dying in the heinous destruction we rained down. Check out the pink tree with its twin trunks entwined around each other. Isn't that the most romantic thing you've ever seen?

Baukis and Philemon

A few years back, Hermes and I decided to test my theory that Iron Age mortals are all driven by craven self-interest. We dressed up as ordinary groveling bumpkins and went door to door in a mountain village atop a tall mesa, begging for shelter. Nobody helped us except Baukis and her decrepit old husband, Philemon. As a reward, I sent the two geezers up the mountainside before we decimated their entire lousy town with one of my favorite retributions, a massive blast of thunder.

Afterward, I blessed the old couple by rebuilding their pathetic little hut, slapping up a Zeusian temple of worship next to it, and giving them the honor of serving as temple janitors for the rest of their dismal mortal lives. I'm just generous that way. I also granted them one wish. They asked to die at the same time. Touching, right? It didn't take long, fortunately—my memory isn't so good these days. When Baukis passed, I took out Philemon too. (Just a flick of my finger was all it took.)

But get this: in the spirit of Aphrodite and eternal love, I turned both geezers into gorgeous pink laurel trees and wrapped the trunks around

each other! I'm pretty proud of that one. Even Hera thought it was a romantic gesture, and that woman can be cold as polar ice.

Palace of Aphrodite

Your tour of the Valley of Eternal Spring ends at the dazzling palace complex on the region's western island, clearly built by Daidalos to suck up to Aphrodite. I mean, come on—the joint is so extravagant and fabulous it's almost embarrassing. A true monument to Aphrodite's eternal vanity! Bring an oxygen tank because the view will take your breath away.

Entry Road

Actually, I'm not entirely sure how a group of schlumpy mortal tourists can access the palace grounds from the mainland. The obvious way is to use the updraft generator next to the colonnaded circular pool at the cliff's edge. But if you're not godly or winged in any way, updraft isn't much use. Maybe you could get a friendly Cyclops to fling you across the gap. But then, there's no such thing as a friendly Cyclops. It would probably just crush and eat you.

I'm sure the Tourism Board has a way to transport its formal island tours across a chasm two hundred feet deep to reach the perfectly sculpted palace grounds. Like I said, breathtaking, right? Follow the winding paved-brick road as it rises beside cascading waters (note the clever clamshell additions) to the first gate. There you can gaze in awe at the great statues depicting Paris handing the Apple of Discord to Aphrodite!

Keep following the road as it curves past statues of lover Adonis, sister-in-law Athena, and a really big (and scary) mother-in-law, Hera. At the top of the ramp you find another statue of Paris holding out the golden apple. Behind him is the palace's highest point, a brilliant domed pavilion with a towering, golden-robed Aphrodite inside. Seriously, other than Mount Olympos itself, I've never seen such a great piece of property.

Fresco Puzzle: Paris and Helen Escape to Troy

As you face Aphrodite's palace pavilion, turn right. See the rock tower across the gap? That's another myth challenge, a fresco puzzle, sitting right on top! The puzzle itself is tough enough to solve, but getting across the gap is the really big challenge here, especially for mortal tourists like yourself. (If you get one of the good demigods as tour guide, she'll hail a winged chariot.) The fresco painting depicts a triumphant Aphrodite admiring the Apple of Discord as Helen and Paris step onto the prow of a longboat bound for Troy.

Constellation Puzzle: The Northern Crown

Before you leave the palace grounds, you definitely want to take a crack at the crazy constellation challenge. Finding the blue orbs to form the stars of the Corona Borealis constellation—"the Northern Crown"—is a mind-boggling task. I don't think you can do it, frankly. But you're welcome to try, unless you get slain by the local poultry first. Don't underestimate the rooster ringleader defending the area. His name is Alektryon, and he's perfectly capable of murder most fowl.

Helen of Troy

We already discussed the intense competition for Eris's nefarious Apple of Discord between the three most powerful Olympian goddesses at my banquet for Thetis and Peleus. What an entertaining scrum that was! As you may recall, Aphrodite won the contest by offering Paris the best bribe—the love of Helen of Sparta. Here's what happened next.

To guarantee her bribe, Aphrodite deployed her son Eros with Paris to meet Helen. When Paris kissed the girl's hand in greeting, Eros quickly nailed her with one of his extra-strength love arrows. Man, Helen fell hard for Paris. It was like a 500-pound sack of gauged mortar hitting the ground. Paris immediately took the love-struck girl home to Troy to meet her prospective in-laws.

Unfortunately, there was a slight problem: Helen was already married. Even worse, she was married to Sparta's King Menelaos, who like all Spartan men was a grim, humorless badass. War was declared, Greek ships set sail, and much grisly death ensued. And sacking. So much sacking. Hey, I like to sack a city as much as the next guy, but the sack of Troy got so appalling that even grizzled Greek Hoplite units held up their hands and said, "No, we're good, thanks."

The Northern Crown

My super-social son, Dionysos, once had the hots for a Cretan princess named Ariadne. The girl had a weird and complicated family history. She was daughter of King Minos and Queen Pasiphaë of Crete, the latter being the unstable woman who so lusted after Poseidon's Cretan Bull that she boinked the thing, resulting in the birth of the Minotaur.

You may recall that our Chryse Island architect Daidalos built the famous labyrinth under Minos's palace to imprison the Minotaur. (He'd also designed the fake cow that crazy Pasiphaë crawled inside to facilitate her truly insane bull-mating activity.) But nobody could actually defeat the Minotaur until a burly Athenian hero named Theseus showed up. Princess Ariadne fell for the big warrior, provided items to help him slay the monster, and then ran off with the guy.

It didn't last long, though. Theseus dumped Ariadne on an island, and that's when Dionysos made his move. He proposed, she accepted, and he gave her a bejeweled crown as a wedding diadem. After the ceremony, we all got drunk and tossed the crown up into the northern sky to commemorate the marriage . . . which, frankly, none of us expected to last much longer than a mayfly.

Alektryon, Legendary Rooster

Alektryon is "herald of the morn"—not a great gig, but as immortal God of Chickens he gets to live forever, albeit as a crowing pest who everybody hates. Poor kid used to serve in the God of War's heavy infantry regiment—a solid, dependable spearman by all accounts. But one night, Ares posted him as sentry outside his bedroom, with orders to let no one pass, and to knock loudly at sunrise.

Alektryon, exhausted from a hard day of practicing his advanced impaling techniques, fell asleep at his post. At sunrise, Helios barged past the snoozing soldier and caught Ares engaging in illicit relations with someone else's wife. (Yeah, it was Aphrodite.) The embarrassed and furious God of War turned the failed sentry into a rooster. Now Alektryon's daily job is to shriek like a banshee when the sun rises until everyone grabs the nearest bedside crockery and throws it at him.

Athena, guardian of the city. With Ares, she loves deeds of war, and the shouting of battle. She saves the people as they go to war and back. Goddess, give us good fortune with happiness! —Homer

Grove of Kleos

Introduction

Ah, the Grove! I really love Athena's region, its year-round embrace of high summer. Tourists may not know this, but the term "Kleos" refers to the heady buzz that spreads after you perform impressively badass things, whether on the battlefield or the civic arena. Kleos means renown, glory, honor, greatness—the perfect name for a land dedicated to Athena's legendary wisdom and tactical military brilliance.

Look, I know parents aren't supposed to admit they have a favorite kid. But it seems kind of ludicrous to deny that Athena is the best offspring ever. What a birth *that* was—she sprang directly from my forehead, fully grown. *Ouch!* But worth it. She's decisive, levelheaded, mature, a fierce warrior . . . okay, maybe a bit judgmental, but always tempered by wisdom. So different from her hotheaded brother, Ares. Always the adult in the room, that girl!

Thus, Daidalos designed a region filled with elegant temples dedicated to the most courageous and resourceful of the Olympian gods. Most virtuous too —no illicit relations with other divinities, demigods, or mortals for this one. As patron of mortal heroes, she bestows them with knowledge, skills, and some really sweet gear.

(Athena's one flaw: She doesn't hold her liquor well. One time she got so hopped up on a kylix of distilled ambrosia she destroyed the entire Greek fleet—the very guys she backed in the war! Next morning she woke and was like, "Where's all my boats?" and we all started making bubbling sounds. My god, we laughed like jackals for weeks over that one.)

Topography

Smaller in area than Aphrodite's sprawling Valley of Eternal Spring, the summery Grove of Kleos features plenty of dense forests, rugged highlands, and deep canyon fissures. Yet, in keeping with Athena's role as goddess of agriculture, the region also includes gently rolling swaths of agriculture, with abundant fields, groves, and granaries. Don't miss the tour of the legendary Moria Tree Sanctuary, where Athena gifted the first olive tree to mortal Greece.

Wildlife

Watch your back for razorback boars, lumbering bears, sharp-antlered deer, hostile chickens, lots of chirpy birds, and the occasional wild Harpy.

Architecture and Design

The countryside is dominated by massive rectangular structures with big broad shoulders—large, imposing temples, shrines, and other compounds celebrating order, perfection, rationality, wisdom, and the glory of victory in battle. Clean mathematical lines and angles predominate, with lots of white and gold detail work.

ᐅᐧ South Central Basin ᐧᐸ

Your tour's point of entry into the grove is at the southern border in its central district, via the main road from Aphrodite's valley. Here, your island trek weaves between stately columns and proceeds under the watchful eyes of the mighty owl on the Goddess of Wisdom statue.

Goddess of Wisdom

From the main gate, your tour veers eastward to the monumental statue of Athena. It rises from an imposing, square-based foundation of stone blocks and mortar, featuring pillars topped with golden owls. Really sets the tone for her region! Note that you can find a Cauldron of Circe at the statue's base, if you feel like mixing up a few potions for the road.

The statue itself is a masterpiece, I must say. Athena is clad in her finest of robes, her kickass Gorgonian breastplate, and her inimitable war helmet. On her outstretched arm sits a pet owl, symbol of wisdom. (I think its name is Larry.) She also clasps her great aegis . . . which, as everyone knows, used to be *my* shield. As Prometheus put it, that aegis "celebrates Athena's dominance in strategic matters of war." What can I say? Like father, like daughter.

Birth of Athena

My first wife, Metis, was a great gal. She produced the emetic that Mom and I fed Kronos to make him puke up my siblings. But later, after I became king of the cosmos, I heard oracular rumors that Metis would give birth to a kid who would depose me. So, one night at a dull party, I took her into a back room and said, "Hey, do that fun fly trick! These losers will love it!" Metis turned herself into a fly. Then I ate her.

But it turns out Metis was already pregnant, and so the kid started growing inside me! (Don't ask. God biology is complicated.) A few months later, I got a super-bad headache. When Hephaistos whacked my head with a hammer (typical god remedy for aches and pains), a grown woman in full battle garb popped out — yep, it was Athena. Then an owl landed on her shoulder. This is the point at which I decided to give up hallucinogenic mushrooms.

Big Lyre

Directly across the road from the statuary entrance sits the region's official Big Lyre. Here you play tunes

learned at the small lyre challenges scattered across the grove to win prizes.

Pegasos Path

From the Big Lyre, head two hundred meters southwest across the grassy meadow to find a majestic cast-metal sculpture of Pegasos, our great winged horse. It's a huge bronze bust of the creature, very striking. What a gorgeous animal! If you've got the wheels, try the navigation challenge Daidalos installed at the statue's base. Sprint westward along the path to a second winged horse flanked by Nike victory statues wielding laurel wreaths.

Pegasos: The Early Years

When the Gorgon Medusa was beheaded by the mortal hero Perseus, she somehow birthed (or "foaled," I guess) a great white winged mount from her severed neck. We named it Pegasos. Some say Poseidon is the horse's father. I can't get my brother to admit it, but it makes perfect sense—he's got a knack for knocking up monstrous females who produce fantastical creatures. It keeps our family lawyers busy.

Anyway, for years, Pegasos roamed the highlands, wild and free. Many mortal heroes tried to tame the great stallion but failed. Legend had it that every time Pegasos stamped the ground, a gorgeous freshwater spring bubbled up on the spot. Gods who wanted custom backyard water features for their vacation homes would chase him around for days, waving carrots. Pegasos, who was a purist about landscaping, ignored them all!

Pegasos and Bellerophon

Like I said, nobody could tame Pegasos on their own. But one night, the mortal hero Bellerophon took a nap in Athena's temple. As he slept, Athena appeared in a dream, handed him a golden bridle, and did some other weird things that I find surprising for a goddess who's supposed to be deeply dedicated to virginity. When the hero woke, that very bridle was in his hands . . . and Athena was standing nearby, looking off into the distance and pretending like she didn't just put it there.

Bellerophon used the charmed bridle to catch and tame Pegasos. Together, man and horse flew off to slay the foul multiheaded monster known as the Chimera. After that, they made quite a team . . . until Bellerophon got cocky and tried to ride Pegasos up to our gated community on Mount Olympos. I had to knock him off the horse's back with a thunderbolt. Guy fell a loooong way. The landing didn't look too good, to be honest.

Western Heights

At the second Pegasos statue, you've actually crossed into the next district, a stretch of rugged coastal bluffs known as the Western Heights. Your tour group now stands at the foot of a massive classical building called the Archives.

The Archives

This monumental stone structure was designed as a research library, a place to study Athena's favorite topics: military strategy and the history of war. It hunkers on a hillside in a terraced complex of square plazas, rectangular pools, and way too many stairs—awfully solid and impressive for something as boring as a library, in my opinion.

Climb the wide entry staircase to a first-level plaza dedicated with statues of the four most renowned and successful mortal heroes—left to right, it's Herakles, Achilles, Odysseus, and Atalanta. Oddly enough,

Daidalos included an empty center pedestal, as if leaving space for a fifth hero. Ha! What a waste. Nobody could match these four badass champions.

At the top, behold the central courtyard of the Archives. Around the perimeter, neatly organized in study rooms, sit all the archived documents. The doors are locked, but who the hell wants to see a bunch of notebooks anyway? Not me, certainly. Note the colorful map of Chryse Island rendered on the ground, though. Nothing like a good illuminated world map, I always say.

Hydra Falls

Now look north beyond the Archives courtyard. See those huge stone Hydra heads snaking out of the sea cliffs? Scary! That's our next tour destination. Descend the Archives back stairs and follow the winding trail. It leads to a viewing platform behind the many-headed

Lernean Hydra exploding like a wriggling, sweat-soaked nightmare from the sheer cliff between the twin waterfalls. Just look at that thing! Can you imagine if, say, a real Hydra was lurking nearby? This is definitely a high point of your island tour. Personally, I could hang out here all day.

Odysseus Myth Challenge: Burn the Hydra Heads!
Adventurous tourists can find an archery pad on one of the terraces jutting from the sea cliff. Fire an arrow through the flaming hoops arrayed inside the fanged Hydra mouths to pretend you're doing the work of Iolaos, sealing shut the beast's necks after Herakles lops off its heads. Feel like a hero? *Ha!* Not even close.

The Lernean Hydra
This serpentine fiend used to hang out in a big lake in Greece's Lerna region, hence its name. To kill the Hydra, you had to kill every single one of its many well-fanged heads. How many heads? Anyone you ask will give a different answer. The discrepancy is probably due to the fact that when you cut off a Hydra head, two grow back in its place! Also, anyone who's actually seen the Lernean Hydra is either dead or a drooling, traumatized loon case. I've consulted with my god council and our best guess is nine heads—eight mortal ones plus an immortal one that could be killed only with a divine weapon.

Herakles and Sly Iolaos Defeat the Hydra
Killing the Lernean Hydra was the second labor that King Eurystheus assigned to Herakles as penance for slaughtering his own family.

Accompanied by his favorite nephew, Iolaos, the brawny hero trekked to Lake Lerna and lured out the angry beast by making fun of its skinny necks. As Herakles chopped off the first few Hydra heads, two grew back in each one's place! Things didn't look good for our guys.

But Iolaos was a quick-thinking kid. He grabbed a flaming torch and, after each beheading, jammed it into the gaping neck wound to cauterize it shut. The Hydra finally lost its heads permanently, one by one. But remember, one head was immortal, and thus couldn't be slain with mortal weapons. Here's where Athena comes into play—the wise goddess had slipped Herakles a special golden sword blessed with divine power. The great gore-stained hero used it to slash off the monster's final godly head and thus slew the beast!

Argo Isle

From the Lernean Hydra head exhibit, look down and spot the small island far below . . . the one with a constellation puzzle in the middle and a longboat docked on the shore. If you're reasonably athletic, it's entirely possible to hop down the cliff's terraces to sea level and take a leisurely swim out to the isle. The ship is a replica of the famous *Argo*, party boat of Jason and his zany crew of Argonauts. Check it out! The thing is tight as a drum.

Constellation Myth Challenge: Argo Navis
Finding and acquiring the five orbs needed to solve this dastardly puzzle is indeed a challenge. But if you can do it, you activate a glittering mural of the Argo Navis constellation and generate a handful of sweet loot.

Building the Argo

When the mortal King Peleus ordered young Jason to find the famous Golden Fleece for him, the kid quickly put together an impressive crew of hero-level warriors. But the prize was stashed across the sea in a land called Kolkhis, so Jason needed a good boat too. Thus, he commissioned Argus, the greatest shipwright of the day, to build a seaworthy ship.

Argus was quite a craftsman, but the journey would traverse some particularly treacherous waters. Thus, as she often does with these mortals, Athena stepped in to help. Under her guidance, Argus designed and built a sleek, sturdy vessel. Athena inspired him to hang sails, batten down hatches, shiver his timbers, and trim the jib while three sheets to the wind. He even made the ship's prow from a piece of blessed oak taken from my own sacred Dodona grove!

In the end, Jason named the boat after its builder, but I think Athena should get an executive producer credit, at least. The Argo proved so impressive that when it was retired, we tossed it into the sky to be memorialized as the constellation Argo Navis.

Athena's Sanctuary

Now it's time to visit Athena's relaxation retreat. Head southwest past the Archives and follow the winding road toward that big Parthenon-style temple you see looming up on the high plateau. That's Athena's Sanctuary. En route you can try a couple of myth challenges, down short side roads to the left.

Lyre Challenge: Mural of the Nine Muses

Accessing this lyre challenge is tricky, but a successful solution opens a secret chamber in the cliff face. Inside, you find the small lyre and a gorgeous wall mural of the nine Muses. From left to right: Clio (history), Thalia (comedy), Polyhymnia (sacred hymns), Euterpe (music), Erato (love poetry), Terpsichore (dance), Kalliope (epic poetry), Ourania (astronomy), and Melpomene (tragedy). Did you know that all nine are my daughters via Mnemosyne? Those were nine of the best nights of my life.

Fresco Challenge: Athena Punishes Arachne

This fresco depicts the moment when Athena had enough of mortal arrogance. Check out that pair of looms rising up behind the fresco. One displays Athena's weave depicting the gathered gods, and the other—the one in tatters—is Arachne's seriously disrespectful version.

Kalliope, Muse of Epic Poetry

Considered the wisest and foremost of the Muses, dear Kalliope is the inspiration for epic poetry, which is considered the highest form of art . . . by epic poets, anyway. Some say she was Homer's inspiration for his masterpieces, the Iliad and the Odyssey. Prometheus keeps telling me that Kalliope "carries inspiration to mortals like leaves on a breeze." I don't get the connection, myself. I mean, what do leaves have to do with it?

But let me tell you, it's not easy being Chief of All Muses, or chief of anything, for that matter. Leadership is an art form most gods and men do not understand. It's lonely up here at the top. So, I relied on Kalliope to help me figure out a fair sharing arrangement when Aphrodite and Persephone were fighting over Adonis. Kalliope's wisdom may be second only to Athena's!

The Weaving Contest: Athena vs. Arachne

This may be my favorite Athena story. My girl may be wise and fair in judgment, but she can really smack down on mortal hubris when necessary. Now, Athena was well known for her elegant fashion sense. She wove her own cloth and was a master of design. But a young shepherd's daughter named Arachne had even more impressive skills in the art of weaving—like, off the charts. She could spin up achingly beautiful patterns and images. Watching her work the loom was mind boggling! Fingers as nimble and precise as a spider's legs spinning its web—and yes, that image occurred to Athena as well, unfortunately.

Anyway, Arachne made the totally hubristic mistake of challenging Athena to a weaving contest. Athena accepted, set up two looms, and the two gals wove wildly for an entire day. The goddess whipped up a flattering image of the gods, looking regal and maybe a bit indolent, but in a cool way. Arachne spun up a similar weave in which we gods were all stumbling around drunk, throwing up, smashing things, having sex with animals, and so forth. Hey, I got a huge kick out of it, but Athena stared for a few seconds, nodded *sagely, and ripped it to shreds. Then she smiled judiciously and turned Arachne into a really gruesome-looking spider. We all know the moral of this story, right?*

Sunken Garden of Atalanta

As you exit the Western Heights district, be sure to pop into the lovely woods just across the bridge north of the Archives. It's an interesting sort of place, featuring a raised rock platform surrounded by a tree-filled sunken garden. Daidalos installed a monolithic rock tablet on the platform that reads: "Stubborn Atalanta. First to strike and first to action." Perfect summation of the fantastic female huntress!

Atalanta the Huntress

Known for her courage, speed, and powerful axe, Atalanta was one of the four truly great mortal

heroes (along with Achilles, Herakles, and Odysseus) in my estimation. Heck of an athlete, this gal—what a runner she was! Abandoned in the Arkadian mountains as a toddler by her father because of her birth gender, the resourceful lass latched onto a she-bear sent by Artemis and learned the ways of the wild forests.

When she finally made her way back to civilized life, Atalanta took stock of the available bachelors and wisely refused to marry any of those clowns. Her legendary skills were finally displayed for all when she joined the Kalydonian Boar hunting party; Atalanta's arrow was the first one to draw blood from the dreaded beast. Later, for some reason, I turned her into a lion. Don't ask why—I was deep into an amphora of Chian red at the time.

◇ ◈ ◇

🔲 *Northwest Highlands* 🔲

This corner of Athena's region features some of the more amazing sites on the entire Golden Isle. Daidalos really outdid himself up here! Cerberos, Medusa, the Furies—some pretty scary stuff.

Hall of Justice

This impressive edifice recreates the legendary courthouse where Athena, in her infinite wisdom, convened the first ever trial. Check out those colossal golden statues of her out front! This is where twelve judges, with Athena presiding, rendered their verdict on Orestes, slayer of his own mother. That's quite a crime among mortals. For us gods . . . yeah, not so much. Most of our mothers and fathers are so abusive it's a crime if you don't kill them.

Fresco Challenge: Athena and Orestes

When solved, this fresco puzzle depicts Orestes bound in chains with one of the Furies hovering overhead, ready to sling freaking snakes at the guy. But wise Athena glares angrily at his captors and points to him, ordering a fair trial that presents testimony and evidence and other stuff that we gods don't need in order to make our infallible snap judgments.

The Trial of Orestes

Orestes, son of the great warrior King Agamemnon and Queen Clytemnestra, was out of town when

his victorious dad returned home from the Greek conquest of Troy. Unfortunately, during the ten-year war, Clytemnestra had taken a lover, Aegisthus, who promptly murdered her husband on his return: Nice work at Troy and now I'm stabbing you. When Orestes got home, he learned of the horrible crime and, like any good son, immediately slaughtered the murderer. But then he slaughtered his mom too. Oops!

Matricide is a big no-no with the Furies (formal name: "Erinyes"), the relentless and horrifying deities of vengeance from the Underworld. They hounded Orestes mercilessly, driving him crazy. Finally, my daughter Athena arranged a hearing before twelve judges, including herself. It was the world's first formal courtroom trial, so whenever counsel would cry out "Objection, your honor!" everybody would yell at him and throw rocks.

Long story short, Athena's vote ultimately acquitted the poor kid. My daughter is so slick she even convinced the Furies to become agents of justice instead of blind vengeance—no more "blood for blood." That's my girl!

Guardian's Hill

Daidalos really knocked this landscape feature right out of the ballpark (a saying my Delphic Oracle contacts tell

me will make a lot more sense in about twenty-five hundred years). The architect sculpted three ferocious dog heads out of a massive rock formation, re-creating the scary visages of Cerberos, Hound of Hades and guardian of the Underworld's gates.

Start by checking out the Herakles stele on the site's entry platform. It lists, in order, all twelve labors of Herakles assigned by King Eurystheus: Nemean Lion, Lernean Hydra, Ceryneian Hind, Erymanthian Boar, Stables of Augeias, Stymphalian Birds, Cretan Bull, Man-Eating Horses, Belt of Hippolyta, Cattle of Geryon, Golden Apples of the Hesperides, and Cerberos. That is one nasty list.

The Twelve Labors of Herakles

After my dear wife, Hera, out of sheer spite, drove the great mortal hero Herakles barking mad, provoking him to murder his own wife and kids . . . well, certain amends had to be made. Not by Hera, of course. Hera never does anything wrong. No, it was Herakles who crawled to the Oracle of Delphi as a miserable supplicant, seeking ways to atone for his bloody rampage. He howled and prayed for Apollo's guidance . . . and Apollo, bemused, thought it might be fun to sentence Herakles to ten years of complete servitude to his goofy cousin, King Eurystheus of Tiryns in Mycenae.

Eurystheus, a gibbering sociopath, immediately scribbled a list of ten "labors" for Herakles to perform—tasks chosen apparently for sheer difficulty, although some of them actually helped people. Later, as it appeared that Herakles might actually complete the list, the king tacked on a couple more impossible tasks, for a total of twelve. Not sure exactly how that's legal, but then, this was a royal court filled with inbred idiots. And to be fair, kings should get to do whatever they want, right? I think we can all agree on that point, at least.

Anyway, I should note that Athena gave Herakles a lot of help in completing his labors. Here's a quick rundown of The Ten, No Wait, Twelve Labors of Herakles, *listed in order:*

1. Slay the Nemean Lion

2. Slay the Lernean Hydra

3. Catch the Ceryneian Hind

4. Catch the Erymanthian Boar

5. Clean the disgusting Augean Stables (in one day, for god's sake!)

6. Slay the Stymphalian Birds

7. Catch the Cretan Bull

8. Steal the Man-Eating Mares of Thrace

9. Snag the Belt of Hippolyta, Invincible Queen of the Amazons

10. Steal the Cattle of Geryon the Giant

11. BONUS LABOR: Steal Golden Apples from the Hesperides

12. BONUS LABOR: Catch Cerberos

◇ ◇ ◇

Catching Cerberos

Every Greek schoolkid knows about this hound. Spawned of Typhon like most monsters around these parts, the three-headed beast serves as the personal guard dog of Hades and keeps its six canine eyes fixed on the Underworld's main gate. A few years ago, King Eurystheus ordered Herakles to kidnap Cerberos as his final labor assignment and bring the creature back to his court. As usual, the king figured it was a totally impossible task. But anybody who knew Herakles could have told him, "Eury, I'd pick up some chew toys and a big leash down at the HellasMart if I were you."

First, Hermes and Athena stepped in to help, guiding Herakles to the Underworld entrance where Cerberos stood watch. Protected from bites by the impervious skin of the Nemean Lion he'd slain in his first labor, Herakles got the big dog in a headlock—I'm not sure which head, but there was a lot of drool involved. Then he hauled it to the surface and presented it to Eurystheus. Funny thing is, a colossal triple-headed dog with razor fangs and horrible breath was the last thing the king wanted scampering around his palace, so he let Herakles take Cerberos right back to Hades.

Temple of Medusa

The next stop is equally chilling. Just southwest of Guardian's Hill, the cursed temple of the fearsome Gorgon Medusa sits on a high cliff. It might seem strange to see a temple dedicated to a hideous snake-haired hag in the Goddess of Wisdom's region, but Athena has a complicated history with Medusa. After all, the goddess keeps the Gorgon's head on her breastplate!

As you climb the temple stairs, note the replicas of petrified mortal warriors, turned to stone by Medusa's gaze. At least I *think* they're replicas. I mean, Daidalos is a stickler for realism in his theme parks, so maybe he hired a few guys and a Gorgon. Whatever the case, these petrified souls remind tourists that life is ephemeral when you're mortal. Cheap, even.

Odysseus Challenge: Athena's Aid to Perseus

Tourists who are insanely skilled with the bow (i.e., none of you) can try this ridiculously difficult archery challenge commemorating Athena's aid to Perseus in his quest to kill the Gorgon Medusa.

The Gorgon Medusa

One of three monstrous Gorgon sisters, Medusa was known as the smart, perky one. With a cluster of hissing snakes for hair and big saucer-shaped eyes that can turn people to stone, she really despised mortals for seeing her as a hideously deformed freak instead of just a dermatologically challenged person. Medusa was once a comely maiden who claimed to be as beautiful as Athena. Then she had a tryst with Poseidon that generated bad feelings in the goddess community. Understandably angry, Athena zapped Medusa with the curse that transformed her. Even her very blood was cursed! Drops of it would turn directly into vile things like vipers, scorpions, and exfoliation brushes.

Medusa's Island

Directly across from Medusa's temple, a dark island thrusts upward like a rocky explosion, topped with twisted trees. Here you can find another pair of myth challenges related to the Gorgon Medusa.

Fresco Challenge: Perseus and Medusa

Piecing together this puzzle depicts the battle of Perseus vs. Medusa. See how he averts his eyes from her? The hero is using that polished metal shield as a mirror to locate and target Medusa without meeting her direct gaze, which would turn him into stone!

Constellation Challenge: Andromeda

Just across Medusa's Island from the fresco is a massive sculpted re-creation of Andromeda chained to a cliff as the sea monster Ketos is about to eat her. Find the blue orbs and place them in the indicated spots on the dimpled platform to re-create the Andromeda constellation. The tale of Andromeda is a great story, but I have to say: You mortals just don't quite get the concept of hubris, do you? Challenging or comparing yourselves to gods always turns out bad.

Perseus Slays Medusa

Athena's curse turned Medusa into a real pain, disrupting trade and terrorizing the entire coastal region. Local leaders sent a warrior named Perseus with a nice monster-killing résumé to eliminate the threat. But Medusa was uniquely dangerous, and the guy clearly needed help. So, a bunch of us gods decided to gear him up, bigtime.

I offered Perseus my adamantine sword, perfectly balanced for beheading; Hermes gave him some winged shoes; Hades provided a helmet from his personal collection; Hera produced a nice backpack to store the head; and Athena gave Perseus a shield so polished he could use it to see Medusa's reflection while fighting, allowing him to avoid her direct gaze.

Setting out to hunt down the Gorgon, Perseus looked like an overequipped riot cop . . . but man, the guy totally delivered on the head! Witnesses say he turned away from Medusa, held up the shield to see behind him, backed toward the angry hissing monstrosity, and beheaded her with a swift backward slash. Then he quickly stashed the head safely inside Hera's backpack.

Amazingly, the Gorgon's eyes retained their deadly stone gaze! In fact, the Greek hero started using Medusa's head as a weapon to petrify foes. Eventually Perseus gave the head as an offering to Athena herself, who mounted it on her breastplate armor as a grim warning to all! (Plus, it looked pretty cool.)

Severed Head Saves Girl!

Not long ago, a woman named Cassiopeia, idiot queen of Aethiopia, bore a lovely daughter she named Andromeda. The young child was truly beautiful, but as Andromeda grew into a striking young woman, her mother ran around foolishly bragging that the princess was more beautiful than even the Nereids, the divine sea Nymphs. Look, my brother Poseidon's court is filled to the brim with Nereids—his wife and daughters, to name just a few. These gals were not happy to hear Cassiopeia's stupid boasts. Just one harrowing session with them convinced Poseidon that a fair divine punishment would be to send a gargantuan and hugely horrifying sea monster named Ketos to brutally shred the entire Aethiopian coast.

After a few weeks of Ketos's grisly slaughter, Cassiopeia consulted a local oracle and learned that only the blood sacrifice of her daughter to Ketos could appease Poseidon. So, like any good mother, the queen chained Andromeda to a seaside rock, left her some snacks, and ran off saying, "Have fun, I'll be right back!" Fortunately for the poor girl, the hero Perseus just happened to be flying past on his winged Hermes sandals after slaying the Gorgon Medusa. He spotted Andromeda, immediately fell in love, and decided to save her. When Ketos arrived, Perseus pulled Medusa's head out of his backpack and aimed its gaze at the sea monster. Ketos turned to stone and sank like a boulder!

❧ Upper Canyons ❧

This pair of sculpted canyons just east of the Hall of Justice feature challenges related to two legendary tales: Jason's search for the Golden Fleece, and the tragic death of the greatest Greek warrior, Achilles. Also: Don't miss the souvenir and concessions stand just off the main road. Everybody knows how kids love to snack on Zeus Pops and toss foam thunderbolts at plush chthonic monsters!

Sacred Grove of Kolkhis

Few things are more fascinating than famous skeletal remains, right? The first thing that draws your eye in this narrow canyon is the glinting golden corpse of the legendary ram Krios Khrysomallos, impaled lengthwise on a long branch of a big oak tree. Here, Daidalos re-creates the sacred grove in Kolkhis where the ram's golden fleece was hung for years before Jason snagged it. The area also features several structures, all part of a sly interactive puzzle.

Constellation Challenge: Krios Khrysomallos, the Golden-Wooled Ram

Solving this star puzzle lights up both the ram constellation pattern and an image of the winged golden ram, Krios Khrysomallos. This is the ovine creature that produced the famous fleece sought by Jason.

> *Jason and the Golden Fleece*
> *Earlier I told you about how Athena inspired the mortal shipwright Argus to build the Argo for Jason and his crew seeking the Golden Fleece.*

When everything was shipshape, the Argonauts set sail for Kolkhis, where the fleece was kept. When they arrived, the local king began demanding favors in exchange for handing over the item. During the negotiations, the king's daughter Medea, a dark-eyed sorceress, fell madly in love with Jason and used her magic to help the dashing Argonaut captain complete the difficult tasks assigned by her father. Among other things, she ponied up a charmed potion that knocked out the huge snaky dragon guarding the fleece.

Once the Golden Fleece was secured, the Argonauts (with Medea) made a treacherous return journey to Iolcos. There, Jason delivered the fleece to his uncle, married Medea, and everyone lived happily ever after . . . uh, well, except the time Jason cheated on Medea in Corinth and she retaliated by murdering their two sons and setting Jason's new lover on fire. (Lesson 101: Never cheat on a sorceress.) And, well, now that I think of it, Jason never regained the family throne, and actually ended up a homeless dude, sleeping under the rotting remains of the Argo. Did I mention that the ship's stern broke off and crushed him to death? So yeah, everyone lived happily ever after . . . who was not in this story.

Achilles Training Ground

This area makes me sad, I'll admit it. Here, in this ravine, Daidalos re-creates the field where the magnificent

Greek hero Achilles trained for battle—with jousting dummies, archery targets, and whatnot. It includes a heartbreaking statue of the great warrior trying to yank an arrow from his heel—the only unprotected part of his perfect anatomy. That arrow killed him! I still can't believe it, and I'll never quite get over the tragedy. Overlooking the ravine is a stele carved with the words: "Confident Achilles, the River Styx protected you from all. But alas, not all of you was protected."

The Achilles Heel

Everybody's heard of Achilles, the greatest of Greek warrior heroes. When Achilles was an infant, his mother, the goddess Thetis, grabbed his heel and dipped him in the River Styx for protection. The waters of the Styx made him invincible . . . all except for that heel, which Thetis neglected to dip too. (What, you couldn't let your kid wade around a few minutes?)

Such a wrecking ball he grew up to be! Swathed in armor forged by Hephaistos, Achilles was the most dominating force in the Trojan War. He slew the great Trojan general, Hector, just outside the city gates—and in a nice touch, dragged the body around Troy's walls a few times yelling insults: "Your bread sucks! Ever tried cumin? I don't think so!" But that Trojan pretty boy Paris fired an arrow from the ramparts that struck Achilles in his unprotected heel, killing him.

Yes, his rage was legendary—when Achilles unleashed his raw anger, he could single-handedly devastate an entire phalanx of Trojan troops. His stubborn pride also affected his own allies— Achilles once grew so angry with King Agamemnon over a "personnel matter" (concubines) that he actually refused to fight for a while. But his eyes . . . such a delicate brow for such a brutal warrior. It just added to the tragedy of his felling by Paris's lucky arrow.

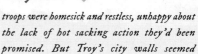

East Lake: *Isles of Odysseus*

Up in the far northeast corner of the Grove of Kleos, a large placid lake shimmers blue around an emerald quartet of lake islands. These isles feature interactive exhibits that celebrate your beloved and clever hero Odysseus. At the lake's west end, you find an entry arch with a stele erected to the great champion that reads: "Cunning Odysseus, you outsmarted a nation, angered the God of the Sea, and won back the heart of your love."

The Trojan Horse

The first island features a huge stylized memorial to the Trojan Horse, well known as Odysseus's most cunning scheme. But did you know that it was the sure wisdom of Athena that inspired Odysseus? Yeah, you forgot that little bit, didn't you? Mortals always try to hog all the credit . . . and Athena lets you get away with it! You people are lucky she holds you in such high regard. See if you can solve the boat puzzle that Daidalos left for you.

The Trojan Horse

Mortal folks love this tale—it's one of your most enduring stories. After ten years of laying siege to Troy had produced nothing but a stalemate, your Greek military leaders were frustrated. The

troops were homesick and restless, unhappy about the lack of hot sacking action they'd been promised. But Troy's city walls seemed impregnable. How to get inside?

Here's where General Odysseus came up with a cunning plan. His engineers built a huge horse on wheels, with a secret hatch underneath. Odysseus and forty of his best soldiers clambered inside, then a Greek regiment pushed the horse to the city's main gate. They left it as a gift offering, a gesture of withdrawal. Then the entire Greek army boarded their flotilla of ships and promptly sailed away over the horizon.

Stunned by their apparent victory, the Trojans hauled the great horse inside the gates and began celebrating wildly. As day turned to night, the drunken revel wound down; citizens and soldiers alike fell into a well-liquored sleep. In the dark, the Trojan sentries on the city wall failed to notice the Greek fleet sneaking back to shore. When all was quiet in Troy, Odysseus and his men slipped out of the horse then unlocked the city's main gates. The Greek army poured into the city, and that was that.

Cyclops Island

The second island is a kind of wildlife refuge, home to a disgusting, smelly Cyclops placed by Daidalos to represent the poor goon who Odysseus famously blinded on his way home from the war. That fellow was named Polyphemos, and like all Cyclopes he's a son of Poseidon. As a result, my brother the sea god doesn't find the story quite as amusing as I do.

Polyphemos Meets Nobody!

After the Greeks sacked Troy, Odysseus set sail for home but got blown off course. The journey back to Ithaca took ten long years as he staggered from peril to peril. Favorite story: After a man-eating Cyclops named Polyphemos trapped Odysseus on his island, our hero got the brute roaring drunk then introduced himself as "Nobody." When the Cyclops fell asleep, Odysseus rammed a sharp log into the monster's one bloodshot eye then slipped away as Polyphemos screamed in pain. All the other Cyclopes came running and asked who did the deed. When Polyphemos howled, "It was Nobody!" his buddies laughed hysterically and all went back to bed.

Penelope's Archery Range

The third island in the chain features a classic archery challenge. To win, stand on the trigger pad and fire a single arrow through a long line of axe handles. This re-creates the shooting contest that Penelope, wife of Odysseus, concocted to distract her myriad suitors as she awaited her husband's return from the Trojan War.

Penelope's Suitors

Gods, I admire this woman! Married to Odysseus, king of Ithaca, she waited faithfully while the cunning warrior traipsed off to the Trojan War for ten long years . . . and then she waited another ten years while he zigzagged and blundered his way back home! Lord, what an odyssey that was, and isn't it a crazy coincidence (not!) that the term for "a long, complicated journey" sounds so much like the guy's name?

Anyway, suitors came at Penelope left and right during those two decades—some wanting her bod, some just craving the king's throne. It got so bad that she came up with a clever contest to keep them all at bay. Anybody who could string her husband's super-rigid bow and shoot an arrow through twelve axes lined up could have her hand in marriage and the kingship of Ithaca. She knew nobody could do it!

Funny thing is, when Odysseus finally reached Ithaca, he snuck into the court disguised as an old beggar to see how things were going. When he learned about the bow contest, he freaked out everyone by signing up and winning easily. Then comes my favorite part: Odysseus tore off his disguise, smiled at all the suitors hanging out in the lobby swilling free drinks and hitting on his wife . . . and then he slaughtered them all! Now that's a truly godlike reaction!

The Lyre and the Aulos

The Satyr Marsyas was pretty talented for a guy with horse ears, hooves, and a tail. His instrument of choice (for music anyway) was the aulos, a double-reed flute, and he was quite good. But he was also ambitious—it wasn't enough that he played all the good clubs and had groupies galore. Marsyas wanted to claim he was the best musician in the world—better even than Apollo! You know, the God of Music. So, the Satyr challenged Apollo to a musical duel. Not a smart move by the horse boy.

Apollo brought his best lyre (I think it was a Fender) and word spread fast. Soon Athena herself arrived to serve as judge, a good role for her. The contest blazed through the night, and it was fantastic! Everyone agreed it was the best music we'd ever heard. In the end, Athena anointed her brother the winner. I'm sure nepotism played no part, nor the fact that Apollo is a god and Marsyas a hubristic mortal freak. To consecrate his victory, Apollo ordered his opponent hung upside down and flayed alive. I believe he used the Satyr's skin to wallpaper his solarium. Haven't I warned you never to challenge the gods?

Grove and Granary District

Eastern Grain Belt

As the district name suggests, this is the farmland of the Grove of Kleos. Golden fields of grain spread in all directions. Remember, don't chat with these local aggies. They're much too busy with all the cultivating and husbandry and whatnot, growing crops and livestock to

present as gift offerings for the praise and glorification of the gods. And also for food, I guess. Apparently, food is important to mortals.

Athena's Gifts
Athena, of course, taught these mortals everything about agriculture—how to till and irrigate soil, how to harvest and store crops, how to mill grain into bread, and so forth. She even inspired the invention of the yoke so mortal farmers could hook oxen to great blades then plow the fields into furrows for seeding. All of which makes me shake my head. Why did I create people who need to eat? Maybe I'll try something more practical with my next batch. How about gills that transform air directly into pizza?

Moria Tree Sanctuary

You can meander south for hours through the billowing wheat fields bathed in torrents of sunlight if you want—but frankly, it gets boring fast. Quaint farmhouses, silos, chickens, wagons . . . seen one, seen 'em all, right? So here your Chryse tour veers westward and heads straight for the looming massivity (what? that's not a word?) of the Moria Tree Sanctuary. This amazing place is an arboretum for olive trees—another great gift from Athena to the mortal race.

Fresco Challenge: Athena's Olives

This fresco inside the Sanctuary structure depicts Athena producing the first olive tree, the original *moria*. Note that behind her, Poseidon's great fountain of water gushes upward from the ground.

Athena vs. Poseidon
One day many years ago, a bustling new town sprang up on the southern coast of Greece. Athena and Poseidon have always competed to provide exclusive patronage to mortal settlements, especially coastal villages. So, both gods rushed to meet the locals, vying for their loyalty. The townsfolk didn't want to alienate either god, so wise Athena proposed a contest—each god would offer a nice gift, and the villagers would decide which one was more useful. The winner would become the village's patron deity, and the loser would bow out gracefully.

Poseidon went first and whacked a nearby boulder with his trident. A spring gushed up in a brilliant rainbow fountain then streamed down past the village. Wow, a water source! Very nice. Ah, but when the villagers sampled the water, they gagged—it was salty! My dumb brother spends so much time splashing around in the ocean playing Marco Polo, he forgot that nobody can drink the stuff.

Next, Athena stepped forward. She tapped the ground with her spear and a magnificent tree sprang up on the spot. It was, you guessed it, the sacred moria—the very first olive tree in Greece! The villagers were ecstatic, voted her the winner, and named their village after her: "Athens." The place grew into quite a city. And many cuttings from that primordial tree would be transplanted into the Moria Tree Sanctuary.

Head due south from the tree sanctuary to the region's final skyline structure. Isn't it gorgeous? That's Athena's Temple, the formal palace where she conducts business. (When she wants to chill, she hangs out in her Sanctuary.)

Athena's Temple

This temple is usually a busy place—people flock to it with offerings for the goddess. The complex includes several side shrines celebrating the truly generous gifts Athena has bestowed on mortals—the yoke, the rake, and the plow. People love ogling tools, apparently. Remember, mortals have to grow stuff out of the ground in order to make bread so they can eat. How sad is that? They reap "grain" and dump it into big storage facilities called "granaries." My poor sister Demeter watches over these ridiculous grain-filled buildings out of the goodness of her heart. I find it all depressing, myself. Everything about being mortal sucks, I tell you.

Inside the main temple chamber you can see the actual sword of Orestes, plus a sweet replica of Athena's aegis. Honestly, it all seems more geared to mortals than gods, but I'll cut Daidalos some slack on this one. Athena really is the people's champion. Folks love her almost as much as they hate Ares!

Athena and Myrmex

More hubris! Athena was once quite fond of a young Attic maiden named Myrmex, a priestess in one of her temples. Myrmex could be a bit saucy, but Athena got a kick out of the girl's bold attitude. One day, in a typical burst of brilliant creativity, my daughter posted a list of gear and gadget ideas to improve lives of mortals. One of these was the plow, which many consider the foundational tool of human civilization. Well, Myrmex was so impressed that she started taking credit for the invention. Big mistake. Athena found out and turned the boastful girl into an ant.

Sibling Rivalry

Quick note on my kids: hard to believe Athena and Ares are actually related sometimes. Athena's such a brilliant tactician—wise in battle but always seeking peaceful resolutions, advocating for war only as a last resort. Meanwhile, Ares sprints unthinking toward the loudest shrieks, wading joyfully into the gore. It's no wonder folks love Athena and hate Ares. The kids even took different sides in the Trojan War—she backed the Greeks, he threw in with Troy. Amusingly, they locked horns a couple times . . . and Athena kicked his ass! A stomping for the ages, let me tell you, with its own soundtrack provided by her personal flautist.

Sing, clear-voiced Muse, of Hephaistos famed for inventions.
He taught glorious crafts throughout the world! Be gracious,
Hephaistos, and grant prosperity. —Homer

The Forgelands

❧ Introduction ❧

My son Hephaistos, God of Fire and Metalwork, has an old saying: "May the light of a thousand forges guide your way." He's never said it to me, but hey, I'm only his father, right? Nobody special. Anyway, this saying certainly applies to his region. Daidalos built this place to be Heph's wet dream—so many workshops, all smoking and steamy and flaring with forge fires, a thousand points of light.

I never see Hephaistos when I visit—I know he's in the Forgelands a lot, but he keeps to himself down in its burning bowels. Occasionally I spot his huge smelly Cyclops assistants lumbering around, but no sign of my son. Everyone tells me he's "the greatest creator to ever plunge metal into flame." All I know is, he's never smiled a day in his life! The kid is racked with torment,

self-induced if you ask me! Thank god he has a father dedicated to making him stronger.

Look, I get it—the kid's mom tossed him off Mount Olympos as a baby. That leaves scars. When Hephaistos landed on Lemnos Island, a couple of do-gooder Nymphs raised him. When he finally returned to Olympos years later, he was already an accomplished blacksmith. He made everyone's armor and weapons—even Ares's, who is very particular about the slaughter factor of his gear. I married Heph off to Aphrodite, which seemed like a good idea at the time. But she cheats unmercifully on the poor guy. It doesn't help that he was always off at his forge crafting weird automatons and such.

Man, if he could just keep his hands off his hammer for a while. Wait . . . that doesn't sound . . . never mind.

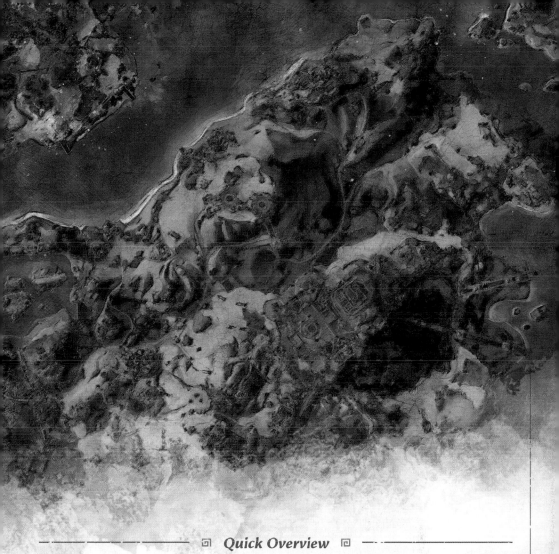

⬚ *Quick Overview* ⬚

Topography

The Forgelands really couldn't be much more different from Athena's neighboring Grove of Kleos, right? Look at all the burnt-orange vegetation—the sparse trees, the arid grasslands and hardscrabble shrubs, the barren rocky canyons and high desert promontories. One might even call it "desolate" if one used such a word regularly, which I don't. I guess all those volcanic vents come in handy if you're building a forge for the ages.

Wildlife

Yeah, the usual boring birds and bears, plus a few horses, notably the rare Khroma breed. One unique addition: the Forgelands features a few prides of lions padding about silently. Magnificent animals! But what you'll see a lot of is creepy metal guys—dozens of them, stumbling around everywhere. I guess you can't call them "wildlife" per se. But they're creatures, they're sort of alive, and you'll have the overwhelming urge to hunt down the bastards.

Architecture and Design

Daidalos really went old school with the Forgelands architecture—almost all Minoan, the older, heavier Greek style. Lots of native stone and clay mixed with copper and marble finish, with primary support provided by reinforced timber. The Chryse Tourism Board tells me I should note the tapered columns, so different from classical Greek colonnade. I don't see much difference myself. It's just a bunch of big poles holding up roofs, right? But sure, go ahead, note the tapered columns. *Wow!*

Points of Interest

⸎ Southwest Canyons ⸎

God of the Forge

Daidalos's monumental statue of Hephaistos is really something. It stands atop a barren plateau, as empty of adornment as my son's head. Yes, Heph hefts his mighty hammer, ready to slam it onto the hot blade that his tongs have pinned to his big blunt anvil, and I'll admit it, every word of this sentence makes me snicker like a schoolboy. Prometheus always says the anvil is "where beautiful things are born." Really? Have you seen his hideous automatons?

Big Lyre

I've never known Hephaistos to be particularly musical. But Daidalos gave him a set of lyre challenges for his region anyway. Here's the Big Lyre of the Forgelands, which sounds like a great title for a bad novel.

Scorpio Rock

I'm not entirely sure why Daidalos found it necessary to carve a huge, harrowing scorpion out of some perfectly lovely white granite boulders, but he did. Good god, look at those pincers . . . that barbed tail! Yeah, I wouldn't go too close if I were you.

Myth Challenges

Daidalos scattered four tricky myth challenges across the stark badlands and canyons of the southwest, each featuring stories related to Hephaistos, of course. One navigation challenge just west of the big Hephaistos statue is devoted to the tale of his Kolkhis Bulls, and another further west is a shrine of sorts to Heph's beloved and seriously strange automatons. Further north, you can follow a dried riverbed to find an archery challenge that commemorates the time Hephaistos battled the river god Scamander. Finally, just east of there, try the Orion constellation puzzle; note the site's great sculpture of Kedalion, servant of Hephaistos, standing on Orion's massive shoulders as he guides the blinded hunter. Great story!

> #### The Kolkhis Bulls
> Hephaistos loves to create robot animals. One of his favorite projects was a pair of massive bronze bulls crafted as gifts for Aeetes, king of Kolkhis. These nasty things would spit streams of fire at anyone who came near them! Years later, when Jason and his Argonauts sailed to Kolkhis seeking

the Golden Fleece, Aeetes set out a list of tasks for Jason to perform before he'd relinquish the prize. First task: yoke the fire-breathing Kolkhis Bulls and plow the fields! The king's witchy daughter, Medea, gave Jason a magic potion to smoke that protected him from their flames. I've smoked the stuff myself, and let me tell you, Medea Gold is a super-trippy experience.

Heph's Automatons

I certainly can't deny that Hephaistos is a wizard at his craft. All the really good gear in Olympos— the really shiny stuff with special whizzy powers—comes straight from his forge. Stuff like Hermes's winged sandals, Athena's aegis breastplate, Eros's bow and arrows, the sun chariot of Helios, the armor of Achilles, and on and on . . . yeah, he crafted all of it. He forged every single throne in our palace! They are truly amazing, I have to admit. Very ergonomic.

But then Heph started building these eerie metal guys he calls "automatons." Sure, it seemed clever at first—they were tireless laborers and did a lot of the grunt work for him. They could operate bellows in brutal heat, and even work metals in the forge fires. But over time, it just got weird. They became his friends. And they were everywhere. You couldn't turn a corner without running into some freaky metallic dude grinning at you like a demented clown.

Boiled Skamander, Anyone?

During the Trojan War, Hephaistos had an epic clash with the river god Skamander. This thin-skinned Potamoi was—like all three thousand Potamoi brothers—born of the powerful Titan water gods, Oceanos and Tethys. (Their family outings must have been brutal.) The river that Skamander inhabited ringed the city of Troy, so he already had skin in the game when the war loomed. But when the incomparable warrior Achilles insulted the river god—something about ramming a Trojan corpse up his tributary—things suddenly got very personal.

Angry Skamander tried to drown Achilles several times by flinging floodwaters across the battlefield. Other gods kept saving the Greek hero. But the best moment was Skamander's totally insane "Fire vs. Water Smackdown" with Hephaistos. Skam tossed a huge tsunami at Achilles but Heph unleashed a thermal blast hotter than Hera's scorn, which is only slightly cooler than the sun's plasma core. Suddenly, it was like a spa! We sat around relaxing in "Skamander steam" for days. It totally scorched the river god and incinerated a few thousand Trojans too. My goodness, it was awesome!

Riding the Shoulders of Orion

Orion was a big hulking hunter, a first-rate slayer of animals whose weapon of choice was a bronze club. The guy was also bit of an animal himself. One time during a hunting party he got drunk and violated the daughter of a king named Oenopion. When the king found out, he had Orion blinded and tossed into the countryside. After a few weeks, the sightless hunter managed to stumble to Lemnos, where Hephaistos worked his main forge.

There, my softhearted (and softheaded) son took pity. He ordered his servant Kedalion to hop on Orion's huge shoulders and guide the hunter east to the great Temple of Helios. (The temple is at the world's easternmost reaches—you know, where the sun rises every day, hauled out by Helios's chariot.) It was quite a journey. Helios is Heph's best buddy and a decent guy . . . for a god. He graciously welcomed Orion into his palace and healed the hunter's stricken eyes.

Well, Orion immediately sprinted away to seek revenge against Oenopion! But the king hid in an underground vault built, ironically, by Hephaistos. Eventually, Orion gave up looking and went hunting in Crete with another one of my kids, Artemis. Unfortunately, the randy bastard made some unsavory moves on her too, so her twin brother Apollo sent down a giant scorpion (cleverly named Scorpio) that stung Orion to death. Afterward, we tossed the big guy's corpse up into the sky, where it twinkles as a constellation today. We flung Scorpio up there too, thinking what the hell, why not? Turns out the sky is a great place to get rid of dead guys or things you don't want skulking around your house, like big scorpions.

Main Forge Complex

This huge industrial complex is one of the biggest and *busiest* places you'll ever see. It's like a small city as Hephaistos and his Cyclops assistants, Brontes and Steropes, hammer out weapons, gear, machinery, and infrastructure like there's no tomorrow. Heph's goofy metal minions come and go in steady streams too, hauling wagonloads of crap all over the island. Huge pistons pump hot air; fire and smoke belch from chimney stacks; steam spews out of grates—it's a real hellhole is what I'm saying. Enjoy the tour, folks! Watch out for open vats of molten metal!

Fresco Challenge: Heph's Workers

This fresco puzzle sits at the base of a tower just south of the massive Forge of the Gods. The finished work depicts Hephaistos and one of his loyal automatons working hot metal on an anvil. Heph created a veritable army of these mechanical helpers to keep his workshops humming along efficiently.

> *Heavy Metal Madness*
>
> *Hephaistos has built a lot of mechanical creatures —fire-breathing bulls and horses, unsleeping watchdogs, giants like Talos, helpers like his Golden Maiden "personal servants" (ahem), and a bunch of really bizarre tripods that stagger around like deformed insects. However, most of his automatons are built as humanoid labor to operate*

bellows and work hot metal in the forge fires. Oddly, they seem to enjoy it.

Cyclops Canyon

This misty canyon drops vertiginously between the enormous Forge of the Gods and its exhaust shafts to the north, those towering ridge-top structures known as Atmos Mechanikos. (We'll visit those soon.) We named this rift Cyclops Canyon because you often find Hephaistos's one-eyed assistant Brontes taking his daily exercise here. All he does is lumber around, pathetically. Nobody joins him, not even his hulking brother Steropes. Nobody I know likes Brontes, to tell you the truth, and I know *everybody*. Anyway, if you want to see a sad ogre stomp around for a while, by all means peek into this canyon during coffee-break hours.

> *Brontes of Thunder*
>
> *Some people call him "Brontes the Bright," which always makes me laugh so hard I start coughing up phlegm. I mean, every Cyclops is basically five hundred pounds of dull rage, right? But I have to admit, Brontes has talent—the guy actually designed my thunderbolt prototype. Also, now that I think of it, he did fight for us Olympians against his own Titan brothers. That showed smarts and earned major brownie points. So, okay . . . good for him. Now if he could just do something about that ghastly Cyclops smell.*

▣ Upper Coast ▣

Atmos Mechanikos

Welcome to the exhaust fans. Whoopie! Can you believe this is a tourist attraction? Okay, so this spectacularly boring pair of platforms is the ventilation system for the Forge of the Gods. At least I think it is. I could be wrong. But frankly, I care so little about forge exhaust that being wrong would almost make me happy. At least you can find a nice Cauldron of Circe nearby to whip up a swig of potion if you're thirsty.

Twin Hammers

After touring the thrilling air vents of Atmos Mechanikos, your outing swings up the main road that runs north. At the fork, veer left (west) and follow the pillar-lined path that cuts through the deep cleft in the coastal headlands. You end up on a high plateau overlooking the sea. There,

a huge stone structure built into the cliffs features a pair of monumental sculptures, each a giant hand wielding a big hammer. Daidalos certainly leaned into the hammer motif for Hephaistos, didn't he?

Fresco Challenge: Three Cyclopes

See if you can solve this fresco puzzle between the big hammers. When correctly rearranged, the image depicts three Cyclops brothers working the forge—Brontes, Steropes, and Arges. (If anybody knows where Arges ended up, please ping me; I'm curious.)

> *Heph's One-Eyed Blacksmiths*
>
> *Two types of Cyclops roam the world. The common Cyclops is big, violent, and not very bright. These brutes eat people, and can be found tending flocks*

almost anywhere. But a special breed of one-eyed blacksmiths, sons of the primordial Titans Ouranos and Gaia, were renowned for their metalwork skills. The three Cyclops brothers Steropes, Brontes, and Arges worked as assistants to Hephaistos in his Forge of the Gods. Some say they crafted Poseidon's awesome trident as well as my own all-powerful thunderbolts. Brontes and Steropes went on to become trusted foremen in Heph's forge. Sadly, Arges disappeared after a murky incident involving a dice game with some centaurs at a local bar.

Gigantomachy Ridge

As your tour continues along the upper coastline, keep an eye out for memorial exhibits depicting events of the Gigantomachy, the war of gods vs. giants for control of the cosmos. It includes a truly awesome ridge-top shrine to me, with a fairly flattering hill carving of the mighty Zeus in mid-windup, ready to toss a thunderbolt. (From the placement of my fingers, it appears I'm throwing a slider.) I don't understand why the small altar right in front of me looks like a chariot wheel, but whatever. Next, follow the trajectory of my toss toward a monumental sculpture on the opposite ridge top — that's the big oaf Mimas, one of the drooling Gigantes brothers!

Odysseus Challenge: A Giant Mouthful

Look for the trigger plate on the hill. When successfully completed, this tough archery challenge gives Mimas the molten mouthful he so richly deserves.

Hephaistos vs. Mimas

Back in the day, some folks didn't fully appreciate the divine omnipotence of Olympian gods. Among those fools were the Gigantes, or giants. They actually tried to conquer us in a war we call the Gigantomachy. Sure, they were huge and nasty... but come on, look at me! My kids are ridiculously impressive too, right?

And yes, that includes Hephaistos. He has his talents. Example: One day we were up on a ridge, trading thunderous blows with a squad of hostile giants led by a real dimwit named Mimas. Heph whipped up a red-hot projectile of smelted iron from his forge and somehow slung it at the trollish leader. This molten missile hit Mimas right in the mouth, terminating his leadership and most of his face too. Then I followed up with the thunderbolt toss. The giant Mimas ended up as a giant pile of ashes, ha!

◇ ◇ ◇

Hephaistos's Workshop

This huge working replica of my son's primary smithy really gets my goat. Here, Daidalos created an exhibit meant to dramatize how Prometheus stole fire from us gods then passed it on to mortals. But I'm curious why Daidalos felt the need to erect a big statue of the lousy Titan thief *actually stealing the fire!* You shouldn't glorify that kind of behavior. Instead, it should be punished via eagle. Also: that's not where Prometheus got fire!

Prometheus the Filthy Immoral Criminal

I've heard false versions of this tale—fake news!—so I'm going to set the record straight. The most widespread one is that Prometheus stole fire from the workshop furnace of Hephaistos and transported it to a bunch of mortal tribes in order to jump-start "civilization" amongst the silly scrabbling human clans of the day. That's why Daidalos built this workshop exhibit.

But the real truth, as I know it in my head (okay, I don't have any physical evidence, please don't tell Athena) is that Prometheus actually pilfered flames from the imported Calacatta quartz fireplace in my luxury penthouse at the Olympos Regency. It must be true, because I can't get that fireplace to light anymore, so obviously someone stole its flame. It had to be Prometheus. Who else could it be?

In response to the theft, I got Hephaistos to craft unbreakable bonds and we chained the fire-stealing Titan lowlife to a granite ledge on King's Peak. Then I devised the perfect divine punishment—every day, a giant eagle eats out his liver. Every day, the liver grows back. The next day, the eagle returns and screams, Snack time redux! *This goes on for all eternity, although I'm thinking of changing it up—maybe target the spleen for a while, just to see what happens. Oh yeah, and I also punished all of mortal humanity with terrible afflictions for accepting Prometheus's gift. Got it, people? Don't ever mess with my fireplace again.*

Quarry Canyon

As your tour rolls through Forgelands rock quarries, past towering cranes and Minoan copper façades built right into the cliffs, please keep in mind that *gods don't have to work at all!* Hephaistos is just weird. Carving colossal blocks out of white granite cliffs, hammering this, hammering that . . . it's all so unnecessary. That's what the Hekatonchires are for! What good does it do to enslave monstrous creatures if you can't sit back, relax, and make them do all the work?

Constellation Challenge: The Charioteer

Near the northern end of Quarry Canyon, look for this interesting Minoan cave complex built right up the cliff wall. At its bottom sits another one of Daidalos's fiendishly clever star puzzles. Find and align the six blue orbs to reveal the Charioteer, a constellation Helios created himself. I'm pretty sure this puzzle commemorates his idiot son Phaethon.

Phaethon the Slacker

This slouchy demigod in baggy robes was an embarrassment to his father, Helios. Phaethon hung out with loser friends who mocked him, so he whined until Helios let him take the family chariot for a spin. Dragging the sun across the sky and grandstanding for his crew, the stupid kid veered through the wrong constellations and clipped Scorpio, knocking a wheel off the chariot. Out of control, the sun chariot dove too close to the earth, toasting a few wheat fields and threatening to burn up the entire world!

Look, somebody had to step in. What choice did I have? Either slay one moronic demigod, or watch all of mortal civilization perish. Fortunately, I never miss—my thunderbolt fastball took out Phaethon for good.

In retrospect, I might have chosen differently if the kid wasn't so annoying. But I figure mortals, given their proclivities, will do a perfectly fine job of incinerating themselves one day. The only sad part of Phaethon's story is that his sisters were so devastated by his demise they let Helios turn them into trees to watch eternally over the lake where he crashed. If I ever crashed and died somewhere, my own sisters would host a little luncheon then quickly divvy up my stuff.

Isle of Talos

Two islands sit off the northeast coast of the Forgelands. The bigger one on the right features an imposing statue of Talos, the colossal automaton Hephaistos built for me to help protect my dear friend Europa on Crete. (Friend, consort—whatever.) Note all the wrecked ships on the shoals—Talos was a damned good guardian! Next, look for the insidious archery challenge on the northwest shore. Finally, be sure to check out the big open-air octagonal arena that dominates the main island.

Odysseus Challenge: Hitting the Nail on the Heel

If you're skilled enough to guide an arrow through a crazy course of hoops, you end up lighting a brazier next to the vulnerable heel of Talos, the gigantic metal protector of Crete's coast. Talos, Achilles—tell me, what is it the Fates love so much about taking down strong guys via their weak heels?

Talos the Mostly Mighty

A while back, I had a little thing with this sweet Phoenician princess named Europa. To seduce her, I had to turn into a bull and hang out in the family herd for a few days. When she finally hopped on my back for a ride, I hauled ass into the ocean and swam to Crete. I made her the first queen of that island and we had some fun, let me tell you.

But the Crete coastal waters can be dangerous, full of pirates and raiders and whatnot. So to protect Europa, I commissioned a monstrous metal defender from Hephaistos. He named the thing Talos, and the big bronze thug circled the entire coast of Crete three times every day. Any hostile-looking ships got hit with tossed boulders. I loved this guy!

Unfortunately, Talos had only one vein filled with ichor, our liquid life source. It ran from neck to foot and was stoppered shut by a single bronze nail on the heel—clearly, not one of Heph's best designs. When the Argonauts passed Crete on their way home with the Golden Fleece, Talos started chucking rocks at them. The Argonaut captain, Jason, asked his new girlfriend, Medea, for help, assuming that a sorceress could handle huge bronze guys. Medea cast a chill spell on Talos, figured out his anatomy, and then plucked out his heel nail. Ichor spilled everywhere and the big guy bled to death. Sad!

Temple of Helios

This is a pretty cool place. Out front, a massive marble sundial is installed on a cobblestone platform. See those horses galloping here and there? That's the Khroma breed, very special animals. It's near impossible to tame a Khroma horse, but you're certainly welcome to try. Inside the temple . . . well, nothing to see here! I mean, there's some gibberish engraved on the floor, but you want to ignore that completely and move along.

Helios the Sun God

First off, Helios is best friends with my son Hephaistos—he's the one who caught Heph's cheater wife Aphrodite bedding Ares. He's a super-reliable fellow, particularly for a son of Titans. Which is fortunate, because his job has to be done daily, like clockwork: get out of bed, hop in the chariot, and tow the sun across the sky. That's why we give Helios a golden temple and pay him the big bucks: no flex hours, no vacation time, no sick days. Skip a day and, frankly, everything goes straight to Hades.

🐚 *East Coast* 🐚

Hera's Golden Throne

Here, your tour runs back across the strait to Quarry Canyon, then follows a steep path uphill toward those tapered pillars. At the top, cross the stone bridge to the fresco puzzle and an exhibit of a really big chair. This chair, of course, is the famous golden throne that Hephaistos crafted for his mother, Hera—a project born of centuries of festering abandonment issues and grievance against the woman. Be sure to climb up on the seat! If you do, the throne rotates to face a tiny island in the distance. *Oooh, a mystery!* Go check it out.

Fresco Challenge: Revenge of Hephaistos

This finished puzzle depicts the moment when Hera sat her ass in the magical golden throne that Hephaistos crafted for her—a throne that immediately turned into an inescapable prison! I love this tale, but man, I'm *really* glad I wasn't there in the moment.

A Special Gift for Mom

I told you how Hera was so embarrassed by Hephaistos's deformed foot and general ugliness that she tossed the boy off of our mountain. I suppose that's the kind of thing a kid never forgets. Hephaistos spent years stewing over this maternal rejection, even after I patiently explained that his mom is sometimes a frightening hysteric and that real men don't get all hurt and nurse grudges. The kid simply ignored my casual sexism and spent years plotting revenge.

Eventually, retribution came in the form of the magical golden throne that Hephaistos crafted for Hera. My wife was so flattered by the gorgeous gift that she plopped down on the seat immediately. Suddenly, magical chains sprouted from its frame and bound my lovely wife to the chair, ha ha! We all begged Hephaistos to free her, but he wouldn't unlock the chains until we promised him Aphrodite's hand in marriage. We had to give in! Poor guy had no idea what he was getting himself into.

Lemnos Island

Don't miss the boat for this island tour! This isn't the real Lemnos Island of course, but it's a clever little replica. Designed by Daidalos, it re-creates the place where Hephaistos lived in exile. Look for the symbolic sculpture—a hammer in a cradle—that commemorates his time here. Cute, eh? If you place it between the nearby statues of Thetis and Eurynome, the two fine maidens who saved and nurtured Heph, you gain access to a lyre chamber for a reward and a musical challenge.

The Maidens of Lemnos
When Hera coldly tossed our lame son Hephaistos off Mount Olympos, he fell miles and miles to the island of Lemnos. There, a sea Nymph named Thetis and her wine club friend Eurynome (one of the elder Oceanids) happened to spot the swaddled baby-comet falling from the sky. They caught the boy and nursed him to health, treating him as their own son. The gals didn't even blink at Heph's Gorgon-faced ugliness! Growing up, he loved those Nymphs and worked on Lemnos as a smith, learning his craft.

Pandora's Shrine

Find this cave on a plateau overlooking the ocean to the east, then solve the puzzle on the cliff face to gain access. Inside, you'll find a mural of gods—Athena, Hephaistos,

Aphrodite, and me—prepping the blue-clad maiden Pandora for her cosmic introduction as the first mortal woman. I tossed in a box and told her not to open it, knowing she would!

Pandora's Box
When I designed my first mortal woman, I asked the other gods for help. I gave Hephaistos the specs and let him tinker with the physical body; Aphrodite did the girl's hair; Athena provided a gorgeous aqua gown; and Hermes came up with her name, "Pandora," as well as her deceitful nature (his specialty). Finally, to spite Prometheus for stealing my fire and giving it to mortals, I had Heph forge a gilded box full of countless mortal plagues—grief, measles, conspiracy theories, herpes, pincher bugs, typhoons, jealous rage, hubris, sinus infections—and gave it to Pandora as a little travel gift.

Look, I totally warned her about it. "Don't ever open this really amazing box," I told her. But once Hermes escorted her to earth, Pandora ripped it open, like, the very instant she hit the ground, and scattered the contents everywhere. Boom! Not my fault. The only thing the girl didn't spill out of the box was Hope.

The Aqueducts

When you're a metallurgist with a forge the size of Vesuvius, you need a lot of water to keep things cool. So Daidalos built a spectacular network of aqueducts to continuously cycle cold ocean water through Hephaistos's main workshops. Take the tour of these multilevel wonders, but be careful, it's slippery up there. Remember, folks, you signed a liability waiver.

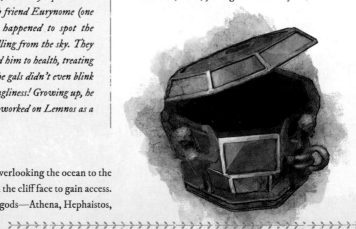

Palace of Alkinous

Check out this spectacular structure built into a soaring stack of rock terraces. King Alkinous ruled his Phaikian subjects with a benevolent hand, but his island was so isolated that his people feared strangers. Thus, it was particularly noteworthy that the king welcomed the shipwrecked Odysseus so warmly, listened to all his crazy travel stories, and gave him ships to sail home to Ithaca. Alkinous also had really big guard dogs, courtesy of Hephaistos. Look for the constellation challenge in the heart of the structure.

Constellation Challenge: Canis Major

Daidalos got a little too tricky for my taste in this star puzzle. Five blue orbs form the famous big dog constellation, if you can acquire them . . . but seriously, these orbs are totally impossible to find.

The Watchdogs of King Alkinous

I gotta say, I like this guy's story. Alkinous was the genial king of the Phaikians, the fellow who welcomed Odysseus into his home on the last stop of the hero's ten-year voyage home from the Trojan War. Alkinous's palace was striking, featuring shiny bronze walls and golden gates guarded by an imposing pair of mechanical dogs—one gold, one silver. These pups were crafted by none other than Hephaistos himself! I'm told Heph's automaton hounds are based on the fierce Molossus, known as the finest breed of guard dog in the world. I wish I had a nice killer dog. I suppose I could ask my son if he'd make one for me, but every conversation with that kid is like a toothache.

Automata Depot

The big Cyclops Steropes works the main forge with Hephaistos, but he also doubles as overseer of Heph's mechanized workforce. This depot houses and dispatches all the automatons that Hephaistos builds. The big central plaza is surrounded by a storage facility for the worker bots. If you see Steropes, tell him Zeus says hello, his lightning sucks, and please stop staring, ha!

Steropes of Lightning

They call this witless gorilla "Steropes of Lightning" because he supplied the sweet lightning zap to my all-powerful thunderbolts. True, it was a nice crafting touch. . . but still, what a dumb name! He and his lumbering brother Brontes both work as assistants to Hephaistos in the great underground forges. They crafted my brother Poseidon's trident too. So, I guess they have skills. But I swear, Steropes looks so stupid you'd swear he's cross-eyed. *Rimshot!*

The Olympian Event Center

Your Forgelands tour ends here, with a wine and cheese reception at the region's southern border with War's Den. Daidalos originally designed and built this venue to commemorate the blessed union of Hephaistos and Aphrodite. God, what a mistake that was. I'm talking about the marriage, not the venue. Although, frankly, the venue has its eccentricities. Staffed by Heph's automatons, the service is prompt, but not exactly personable. They're like, *May I procure you another fermented grain libation, meatbag?* The house band is pretty amusing, though.

War's Den

·} Introduction {·

It's always sad when you've got a kid that nobody likes. Hera and I have been telling Ares forever that he needs to lighten up. Mindless fury is fine when you're hacking up a Titan, but come on . . . all the time? I mean, just because you're the God of War doesn't mean you have to slaughter everyone who gives you a sideways look. I'm certainly not one to wallow in self-reflection, but let's face it, always acting impulsively leads to bad choices. Like sleeping with your brother's wife, for example. Repeatedly.

Look, I certainly get Aphrodite's attraction to Ares. The guy is ripped. When he whips his four-horse chariot across a battlefield, strapped in his adamantine armor with a sword in hand, he cuts a hell of a figure. But he's so reckless, always starting wars for no good reason. And he takes himself so seriously! As a father, I consider it my job to knock him down a notch. I make jokes. It's all good fun, right? I just wish he could be more like his sister Athena.

Anyway, Daidalos certainly built War's Den in the spirit of its patron god. This region suits Ares well. Check out all the massive granite sculptures of giants, flailing and perforated with ballista bolts. Fun!

◇ ◇ ◇

Quick Overview

Topography

This bleak landscape is the kind of place only a warmonger like Ares could love. Stark plains and plateaus coated in apocalyptic orange dust . . . great gashes of canyonland leading nowhere . . . an almost total lack of trees and vegetation. It smells like somebody burned down a castle filled with trapped bodies. Really, the whole place is just like Ares himself—messy, tumultuous, dangerous, and in need of a decorator.

Wildlife

War's Den is home to lions, horses, spike-backed boars, plus a species of really annoying crows. You also see a lot of wild jousting dummies.

Architecture and Design

Daidalos really leaned in hard on the military motif here. The region is filled with Mycenean forts and citadels, typical of warlike people—enormous Cyclopean stone block fortifications and cobblestone yards, all built of ashlar masonry, with crossbeamed interior walls covered with plaster. The massive Fortress of Ares is so big it covers nearly one-third of the entire region!

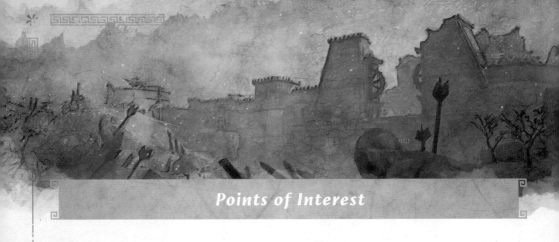

Points of Interest

Northern Fortifications

Entering War's Den from the Forgelands is a slightly weird experience. I know Daidalos built these lands based on themes relating to patron gods. But why did he feel the need to make the northern gate pass through three lines of fortified walls? Look, I know Heph and Ares aren't exactly buddies, but they're brothers and ...well...okay, there's the Aphrodite thing. Maybe it makes sense. In fact, maybe adding a fourth wall wouldn't be a bad idea. These guys hate each other.

Border Canyons

The first thing you see is Dragon's Mesa rising up right in front of you. Our tour will circle back to that site later. For now, turn right and follow the road that meanders west through the canyons beneath the military outposts and fortifications lining the region's northern border. It's a lovely trek, if you happen to like grit. The stuff gets in everything...your eyes, your beard, your girdle. Terrible! The road curves past boring walls and forts all the way to Westgate Ward. Note the towering Ares statue rising up in the distance to your left. We'll get there eventually, too.

Caves of the Seven

Don't miss this Thebes-themed star puzzle installed in a bastion just north of the first crossroads. Technically, the constellation Serpens or "the Serpent" celebrates Ares's big slimy snake—the protector Drakon Ismenios—that once guarded the God of War's personal bathing spring. But the puzzle's seven-cave network—plus the seven shields lined on the back wall—also refer to another famous story, the tale of Seven Against Thebes.

Keep following the road west past the fire-topped signal columns marking the rugged route. Eventually you weave along a river canyon until you reach the gate that connects War's Den to Aphrodite's region.

Seven against Thebes!

Years ago, a generation before the Trojan War, a guy named Oedipus became king of Thebes. He was a good king ... except for the fact that he gained the throne by killing his own father then marrying his mother. That sucked. So, he went into exile and left the throne to his two sons, Eteokles and Polynices. They tried taking turns as king, but when it was his turn, Eteokles kicked his brother out of Thebes.

Well, Polynices wandered to a place called Argos, where people are called Argives for some reason. He made seven badass friends who were all champions of one sort or another. One was unbeatable in board games; one could kill anybody with tongs; another won all the drinking contests. After Polynices told them about the Thebes situation, the seven champions decided to help him regain the throne. They formed an Argive army, each with his own regiment. This was perfect because Thebes had seven gates. So, each Argive champion led an assault against a different gate.

Now, here comes my favorite part of the story: They all lost and were butchered. All seven of them. Not a single Theban gate fell! Then the two brothers, Eteokles and Polynices, met on the battlefield for a one-on-one duel ... and they killed each other! How's that for an unexpected and awesome ending, champions and kings hitting the ground hard, all across the board?

West Gate

Here's the gate connecting War's Den to the Valley of Eternal Spring. Look for several myth challenges as you head northwest toward your next **tour** stop, Giant's Fall. Each one has its own tale to tell, so check them out!

Small Lyre Challenge: The Trojan Memorial

This exhibit is dedicated to all the brave warriors of Troy snuffed out in the war. I guess it's poetic—a bunch of extinguished braziers. Frankly, I couldn't care less who wins mortal wars. The only reason I ended up rooting for Troy, sort of, is because Hera borrowed Aphrodite's magic girdle to seduce me into backing her side. She had me singing "Fight On, Trojans!" all night.

Fresco Challenge: Diomedes Wounds Ares

This amusing fresco depicts a really, really great moment in the Trojan War—one of my favorites, I must say. It shows Athena helping the boy wonder Diomedes stab Ares right in the freaking stomach! Check out the stunned look on Ares's dumb face.

Odysseus Challenge: The Moirai

Follow the road that circles Giant's Fall and veer left at the herm marker. Then climb up the narrow butte past a set of three stone towers representing the weavers of life and death known as the Moirai. An archery trigger plate sits atop the final tower.

Hey, Can You Help Me Gut Your Brother?
Not many mortals could take a slice of god flesh in battle—Herakles is the only one that comes to mind—but Diomedes was a special kid. Of course, he needed Athena's help; no mortal beats a god without godly backup. In this case, a battle was raging outside Troy's gates, and Ares (as always) was wading ankle deep in the gore of fallen Greek foes. But suddenly this wild Greek chariot comes screaming around a corner in a power slide— wow, it's Diomedes! He starts showing off a bit, popping wheelies and such.

Well, Ares just sneers and slings his spear right at the kid's head. It looks like a sure kill-shot but suddenly the spear stops in midair. Guess who? Yeah, your sister, chump! Then, as Diomedes dashes in close and thrusts his spear, Athena grabs the shaft and guides it in. Wait, did I just write

---

that? What I'm saying is, she wrapped her fingers around Diomedes's lance and steered it right into her brother's midsection and, good Hermes, what am I saying? I'll just tap out here and hope you get the gist.

Witnesses have officially testified that, when stabbed, Ares "screamed with the voices of ten thousand men." But folks, I'm here to tell you that description is about twenty thousand voices short. What a howl! I personally hauled Ares home and listened to him whine like a little boy the whole way. It sounded like every family vacation we ever had: Dad, it's not fair! Dad! Dad! Make her stop poking me!

What the Fates Decree
My three daughters known as the Moirai are straight-up bosses, just like their Titan mom, Themis. Also known as "the Fates," these iron goddesses control the destiny of every mortal. Clotho begins each new life by spinning its thread. Lachesis measures the life thread to determine how long it is. Atropos cuts the thread at the end—the predetermined moment of death. Their decisions are so final that even the gods must submit to what the Fates ordain—no bargaining or negotiation allowed. That means all of us, including yours truly. You'd think a father might have some influence, but no, not with these girls.

Giant's Fall

As you cross War's Den, you see a lot of unsettling hill carvings of massive suffering giants. Why? Because we kicked their ass, is why! The Gigantomachy, our war against the giants, was a brutal affair. But it ended at Giant's Fall, our stronghold where the giants' last-gasp assault broke like a foamy wave against granite cliffs. This exhibit marks the beginning of the glorious age of the Olympian gods. First, we hammered the Titans and their pet monster, Typhon. Then we broke the insolent Gigantes tribe, the giants of legend. Now we alone rule. Get used to it!

The Gigantomachy
The giants were an aggressive tribe of one hundred hulking goons. Like so many powerful and stupid creatures, they wanted to rule the

cosmos. But the problem with being powerful and stupid is that, sooner or later, you run into someone who's powerful and smart. Like, say, an Olympian god named Zeus? Does that name ring a bell, people?

Look, the Gigantes tribe made a hard run at ending the rule of the gods, and defeating them wasn't easy. They threw a lot of boulders at us. That wasn't pleasant. Poseidon had to slam an entire island on the head of one tough giant named Polybotes. But eventually, we figured out how to use the huge ballista launcher at Giant's Fall and skewered a lot of those big boys.

Potting Ares

Ares certainly had issues with giants, as did we all. But he had one particularly embarrassing encounter. Twin sons of Poseidon named Ephialtes and Otos grew into colossal and somewhat dimwitted giants. I won't lie—they were huge, terrifying creatures. Nearly invulnerable. Not even my own thunderbolts could take them down. They were also arrogant oafs . . . at one point even laying siege to Mount Olympos after locking our illustrious God of War inside a bronze pot! Trust me, it was as amusing as it sounds.

Fortunately, both Ephialtes and Otos were totally obsessed with shagging Artemis. She's a smart cookie, so she transformed into a doe, taunted their manhood, and hopped between them. The big imbeciles simultaneously flung their mighty spears at her, skewering each other, and that was that. Both brothers are chained to pillars in the Underworld now. (Sometimes, just for fun, I go down and throw stuff at them.) You know, I can't remember how we got Ares out of that pot. We were all laughing so hard!

Big Lyre

Almost unbelievably, Ares is a bit of a musician. As a kid he used to drive us insane by running around the palace blasting his salpinx, mostly the "Full Frontal Assault!" bugle call. Of course, you're not going to get that kind of melodrama from a lyre. But Daidalos is clearly fond of musical puzzles, so he dropped in a Big Lyre next to Giant's Fall and added a few small lyre challenges scattered around the region.

God of War

Yeah, Daidalos chose a perfect Ares pose for his monumental statue. Look at that thing! Striding forward . . . the only direction Ares cognitively grasps, salpinx to lips, trumpeting the battle charge. Sword up, ready to eviscerate puny foes. And I can tell you this, too—there's not a single thought in his head. But he's happy! Athena calls him "the God of Joyful Slaughter" and she's exactly right, as always.

Two Warriors Shrine

From the God of War, your tour heads north where a big installation with a star puzzle squats on the next mesa. Note the two massive warrior statues wielding flaming swords. At left, Ares also hefts a battle axe, ready to cleave things. At right, a delusional victim thinks his ridiculous little shield will protect him. Should be quite a fight! Just kidding, Ares will inflict heinous wounds, howl with savage delight, and take pleasure in defiling the corpse. The Spartans absolutely love him, of course. The rest of us are, like, "Nice win but no thanks, we'll pass on the trophies you hacked off bodies."

Constellation Challenge: The Altar

Find the blue orbs and assemble them into Ara, the constellation that commemorates the famous altar where we gods formed our wartime alliance for the ten-year Titanomachy. Note the smoke rising from our offerings—you can't have a decent altar without burning animals and incense. Poseidon always tries to sing sea shanties too, but we usually just stare at him until he stops.

Ara the Altar

When we Olympians decided to overthrow Kronos and his Titan cohort, I had each of my fellow gods swear an oath of allegiance to my leadership at this altar. After we won, I tossed Ara into the sky in memory of "our" godly victory. (Hey, it was mostly me, but I'm big enough to share accolades with my underlings.) Now, every night I look up at Ara's twinkling stars and remember just how fantastic I am at this head-god thing.

◇ ◇ ◇

Fort Gyes

For some strange reason, this godforsaken outpost is named after Gyes, one of the three monstrous Hekatonchires brothers—the fearsome Hundred-Handers—born to my grandparents, the ancient Titans Ouranos and Gaia. (I guess that makes the Hekatonchires my uncles, which is just weird.) Take a cursory look if you want. It has one of those huge ballista siege weapons. But more interesting is the navigation challenge that starts just south of the fort.

Navigation Challenge: Sisyphos and Thanatos

Trigger this run-jump-glide challenge and then run, jump, and glide your way up to the shrine. You can glide, right? If not, maybe your demigod tour guides can hurl you.

Shrine of Sisyphos and Thanatos

Daidalos's memorial to these two guys is just past the Nike statues where the navigation challenge ends. Climb the stairs and peek inside both chambers to see the shrines. Very nice mural work here! I'm particularly fond of the Sisyphos pic—one of my favorite cruel torments, almost as good as the one I dreamt up for Prometheus.

> ### Sly Sisyphos Punks Thanatos
> I'll tell you the moral of this story right up front: never get in the way of Ares's sick love of carnage. Sisyphos was a devious guy who used to annoy me quite a bit during his days as king of Corinth.

> Thus, when it was time for him to die, I sent my winged minion Thanatos, God of Death, to escort old Sisy down to Tartaros with orders to shackle him to a rock for all eternity.
>
> But when they arrived, Sisyphos acted confused and said, "I'm not clear on this shackling procedure, could I get a demonstration?" Thanatos complied—wow, the guy really is none too sharp—slapping the cuffs on himself. You can see why we put him in charge of dead people. Sisyphos grabbed the key and split, laughing like the jackal he is.
>
> Problem was, with Thanatos chained in Tartaros, nobody could officially die! (I know, I know, it's a pretty bad systemic bug.) Out on the battlefield, Ares was dishing out his usual butchery, but the horribly mutilated corpses would just stand up, flip him off, and walk home laughing (if they still had throats). Man, was Ares furious! When I explained the situation, he immediately rushed down to hell, freed Thanatos, and then hunted down Sisyphos, who was hanging out in sunglasses at a gyro stand in Delphi.
>
> This time, I came up with a really nasty Tartaros Special for Sisyphos. Every day, he pushes a super-heavy boulder up a hillside. Every time he reaches the top, the rock rolls back down, so he has to do it again. He can't just refuse the task, because then the Furies come for him. Trust me, you don't want that. I'd rather eat out my own liver than have Furies shrieking at me.

◇ ◇ ◇

🔲 *Dragon's Mesa* 🔲

Protector Drakon Ismenios

I'm sorry, but this is one of the saddest things I've ever seen. I know Ares loved this overgrown water snake, but really, hauling its carcass to Chryse from Thebes? The bones are certainly quite a spectacle, but I hope you have a bandana to pull across your face, because the smell is about as ripe as you'd expect a massive dead thing to be.

Odysseus Challenge: Water Dragon of Thebes!

Out of respect for Ares and his nonstop mourning for the Drakon, I won't crack any snake-related jokes here.

> ### The Drakon Ismenios
> Our savage God of War really loved this hissing menace—when it was young, he'd walk it

> around like a pet, laughing fondly as it set fire to nearby suburbs. (Property values really dropped.) Eventually, it grew into an immense green-eyed monster and spent many years guarding a sacred spring devoted to Ares. When the dragon was killed by the mortal adventurer Kadmos (more on that later), Ares mourned deeply and transported its bones here to War's Den. Whenever its skeletal teeth drop to the earth, they magically sprout into heavily armed soldiers called Spartoi, the "sown men."

> ### Kadmos and the Spartoi Soldiers
> Kadmos was a fine young man, for a mortal. On a journey in search of his missing sister Europa—

the young woman I seduced by disguising myself as a gentle white bull who smelled of flowers, one of my better pickup moves—Kadmos and his men ran into the Drakon Ismenios, the terrifying serpentine monster guarding a spring belonging to Ares.

In the ensuing fight, Kadmos lost some of his warriors but managed to knock out a few dragon's teeth. In a truly twilight-zone kind of moment, the falling teeth struck the ground and, being sharp, were implanted into the earth. After a few moments, each tooth sprouted up into a tough armored soldier!

Known as the Spartoi, these "sown men" joined up with Kadmos and helped him found the city of Thebes, not far from the Drakon's spring. In fact, those first Spartoi became city elders. I think a few of them became dentists too. And Kadmos, first king of Thebes, became one of the most renowned beast slayers in all of Greece.

Shrine of Kyknos

Just east of the Dragon's Mesa, Daidalos built a bunker complex dedicated to Ares's son Kyknos, a famously bloodthirsty and cruel kid. (What a shocker, right?) Why does Kyknos get his own exhibit? Not really sure. Enjoy the tour, keep an eye out for the small lyre challenge, and watch out for purple lasers of death.

Navigation Challenge: The War Horses

Ha! I've yet to see anybody beat this racing challenge on foot. You need a horse, which plays into the theme Daidalos developed for this attraction. Look around for a speedy Krater mount before you trigger the start plate! The finish line area includes a replica of Ares's fearsome chariot, as well as a tribute to the immortal, fire-breathing war horses that pull the legendary vehicle.

Ares's War Chariot

Nobody would question that Ares is a mindless, savage warrior. But I have to admit, the guy also has a surprising knack for building his brand. Take his famous war chariot, for example. See the golden corpse-eating bird perched on the carriage? That sends a clear message. When that vehicle rolls onto the battlespace, enemies quickly question their commitment to the fight.

Scary Sons of the War God

Ares and Aphrodite have had quite the ongoing affair behind Hephaistos's back, producing a string of kids over the years. Some were nice, like Harmonia. Others were . . . less nice. In particular, they had a couple of sinister boys, Phobos and Deimos, who scare the holy bejesus (whatever that means) out of even me. As it turns out, their creepiness proves quite useful in battle. They work in tandem, and their shtick is brilliant!

Before any military engagement, Deimos saunters casually through the enemy ranks, grinning like a skeleton and whispering super-grisly rumors about his dad's sadistic plans for defiling their corpses. Then, as the battle starts, his brother Phobos takes over. Shrieking like an entire platoon of Erinyes, Phobos swings Ares's terrifying war chariot in circles around enemy formations, spreading horror and panic. I tell you, I've seen battles end before they even started, thanks to these two ghouls.

Hippolyta's Temple

Daidalos designed this impressive complex of structures to honor my favorite tribe of granddaughters, the Amazons. The whole place is basically one big puzzle that unlocks an archery challenge. Delayed gratification isn't my thing, so I've never tried to solve it. (I just look up the cheat codes.) But whether or not you take a crack, be sure to stroll around the place, checking out the awesome Amazon warrior shrines. Note the big one depicting mighty Queen Hippolyta on horseback. She's about to deliver an Amazon package right to some enemy's thorax!

Odysseus Challenge: Bow of the Amazon Queen

Ooooo, this is a crazy one! I don't think even Hippolyta herself—whose archery skills are said to rival those of both the great hero Atalanta and the God of Archery Apollo—could wend an arrow successfully through this course of hoops. But maybe you can. Success brings rewards and triggers the tale of "Hippolyta's Girdle" as told by your tour guide.

> #### Amazon Fulfillment Center
> *This regal tribe of ferocious female warriors—no men allowed, except for breeding purposes or comic amusement—is absolutely unmatched among mortal clans in strength, agility, and skill in the military arts. A squad of Amazon archers on horseback is a sight to see, let me tell you. Unless they're coming for you. Then you really don't want to see them. Some say Amazons only raise daughters and send off any baby sons to their fathers . . . unless they've already killed the fathers. In that case, they just send the kid over a waterfall. It's a bit harsh, but you have to admire people who don't compromise their values.*

Hippolyta's Girdle

The Amazons, all daughters of Ares, are a formidable tribe of female warriors and hunters, so you can imagine how badass their queen is. Queen Hippolyta wore a magic "girdle" that enhanced her combat skills—a gift from her father. (Getting a girdle from your dad might seem awkward, but it's basically just a waist belt.) So, the annoying King Eurystheus decided to make "Steal the Girdle of Hippolyta" his ninth labor for Herakles because he wanted the belt for his own daughter.

Everybody feared Herakles would battle Hippolyta for the girdle . . . likely to be a titanic fight, for sure. But shockingly, the musclebound brute just asked nicely and the Amazon queen simply handed it over. During the transaction, Hera tried to stir up controversy among the Amazon troops, but to no avail. Not many legendary Greek tales end with such diplomacy and anticlimactic lack of gore!

Ambrosia Islet

See the tiny dab of rock just a short hop east of the main island? If you have a strong desire for a dose of Amazon-scented ambrosia, this islet is your delivery center. The return policy is reasonable, I hear. Enjoy the swim.

 Ajax's Fort

When Ares was a kid, he spent a lot of time in his room playing with toy soldiers. Hera and I used to watch him repel imaginary assaults, impaling attackers on rows of palisades and stringing up their little corpses by the ankles to feed the buzzards. It was so cute! Then, when Ares grew up, he oversaw construction of the most impregnable fortifications in the cosmos—ironically, with the help of the brother he was cuckolding regularly, the great forge-master Hephaistos. Isn't that wild? Families are complicated sometimes.

Entry Bastion

Here on Chryse, Daidalos has constructed a truly impressive facsimile of the God of War's main Olympian fortress. He named it Ajax's Fort, which I don't quite understand since both Ajax the Great and Ajax the Lesser were Greek warriors (as was Ajax the Middling, I believe) whereas Ares fought on the side of the Trojans. So why name your fort after enemies? Maybe because you want to skin them, disembowel them, and build a fort inside their bones? Classic Ares. Anyway, Ares likes this fort so much that, I swear, he spends more time here than back on Mount Olympos. This entry bastion is the first layer of defense.

Ajax the Great

This guy was a brave and powerful Greek soldier who played a big role in the Trojan War. Trained

by the great centaur teacher, Chiron, Ajax was also a close friend and cousin of Achilles. Some called Ajax "the Bulwark of the Greeks" although he kept telling them, "Guys, just call me the Jaxman." He fought two long, brutal duels with Troy's greatest warrior, Hector, and both ended in a draw!

Sadly, it was Ajax and Odysseus who took on the terrible task of retrieving the body of Achilles after the great warrior was killed by Paris's arrow. Afterward, the two quarreled over who got to keep their friend's armor, forged by Hephaistos, so you know it was good. Achilles's mother, Thetis, awarded the armor to Odysseus, and Ajax was so distraught he fell on his own sword in protest. I told him to just find a good civil litigator, but he wouldn't listen! Always the drama queen, that Ajax.

Ajax the Lesser
Nice designation. The fellow leads his Locrian troops against Troy in the wars, wins some nice battles, and they call him "the lesser"? On the other hand, the idiot did storm Athena's temple and violate a Trojan priestess, Kassandra. Nobody does that in Athena's house. When his Greek allies let Ajax slink away without punishment, Athena conjured a storm to wreck the Greek fleet. I'm telling you, never cross that girl.

◇ ◇ ◇

Rest of Fort
There's a *lot* of good fort stuff here. I've plundered its spoils a few times, seeking fair payback for raising that savage hellion of a kid. Keep your head on a swivel as you proceed from chamber to chamber, banquette to banquette, parapet to parapet, embrasure to embrasure—all those fort places about which I don't know or care much. (If you've seen one embrasure, you've seen them all.) Hey, I hear Ares has a treasure room, though. That might be fun to see.

Eventually the tour ends up outside the fort's massive walls on a stone platform atop a precipitous sea cliff, overlooking a heart-shaped island far, far below.

Apple Isle
Too bad there's no way a mortal can leap off a cliff and fall hundreds of feet into the ocean and then swim treacherous coastal currents. Because if you could, you might explore this island. Not sure how Daidalos sculpted an entire island into a perfect heart shape, but the place is a touching tribute to the forbidden love (sort of) shared by Ares and Aphrodite. The isle includes a fresco puzzle and a shrine to Aphrodite with a giant apple offering at her feet. I worry somebody will steal that apple, but only a jerk would do such a thing.

Fresco Challenge: The Divine Triangle
You know this story well. The completed fresco puzzle shows Aphrodite and Ares entwined in her private bower as her poor suffering husband (Ares's poor brother) sits outside, anguished. Grab the popcorn!

King's Peak

🝔 *Introduction* 🝔

Before your Chryse tour group returns to the Port of Entry at Clashing Rocks to be shipped back to whatever godforsaken land you call home, be sure to take a lingering look at that huge snowy mountain rising to the north. That's King's Peak, my favorite region. Isn't it stunning? Too bad it's inaccessible to the standard mortal. But it's so amazing I can't let you leave without getting a glimpse of its glory.

Non-godly people can't go to King's Peak for several reasons. You'd die in seconds, for one—Daidalos made the place too frigid for mortals to bear, a nice move by

my *dearest* architect. He knew how much Hera and I treasure privacy in our various retreats and compounds and palaces. I guard my me-space and me-time jealously. Any mortal who can avoid freezing to death on King's Peak (and you can't) would end up getting a thunderbolt in the face.

But I'm not above sharing the supreme awesomeness of my godly digs with lowly mortals. So, this chapter gives you a peek at my peak, ha! God, I love wordplay. Hey, don't tell Prometheus I said that. Anyway, let's take a virtual tour, shall we?

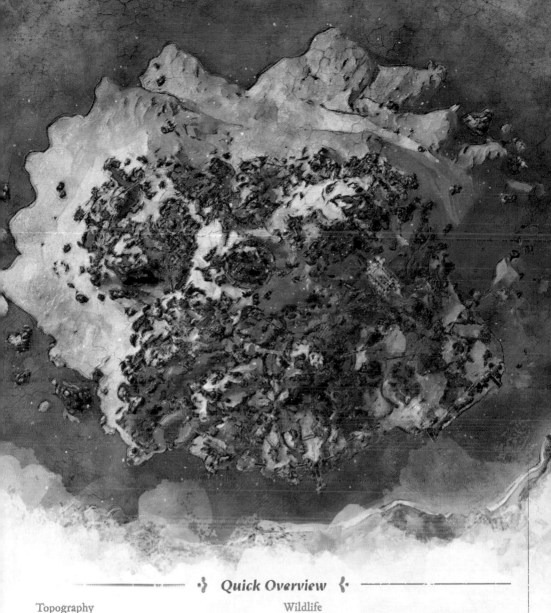

Topography

King's Peak is a ginormous frozen mountain sitting on an island separated from the rest of Chryse by an ocean channel and towering sea cliffs. The place is inapproachable from the north and only barely approachable from any other direction. My mountain's jagged crests are icebound and forbidding to all who are not gods or monsters or great beasts.

◇ ◇ ◇

Wildlife

Again, nothing but monsters or great beasts could live here. And I don't allow monsters. So, no wildlife to see here, except maybe a handful of bears.

Architecture and Design

Epic and hostile, just the way I like it up here at the top of the world. Lots of really big Titan sculptures suffering gruesome defeat, slain as they fail miserably in their attempted ascent of my citadel.

King of Gods

Five different bridges run from the main island across to King's Peak, which is four more bridges than seems necessary, if you ask me—and Daidalos *didn't* ask me, although I'll cut him slack—he wanted Chryse to be a surprise gift. If you cross the center bridge from the Grove of Kleos—and you can't, because you're a mortal tourist, remember, so don't try—the first really cool thing you see is the monumental war eagle sculpture, King of Gods, ripping the snot out of a big stupid Titan trying to climb my mountain. What a masterpiece! It may be my favorite monumental sculpture, ever. Note that Daidalos put a Cauldron of Circe and the region's Big Lyre right next to the big bird.

War Eagle = Me

Some ancient tales suggest that the great war eagle was a creation of Gaia and worked for me during the Titanomachy, fighting Titans. But I'm here to tell you that's not exactly the case. The fact is that I, Zeus, head god, master of the cosmos, am the war eagle. Yeah, I turn into a big freaking eagle whenever I feel like it, and hang out with other huge eagles . . . like Carl, the guy who eats Prometheus's liver every day. He loves his job! Anyway, eagles rock, and that's why I always put a golden one on my war standards.

◇ ◇ ◇

Punishment of Atlas

Work your way up the center of King's Peak to find this outstanding rock sculpture of Atlas holding up the sky on his shoulders. Gods (and maybe a hero or two) who can actually reach this spot will also find a small lyre tinkling seductively in front of a statue of Pan playing his pipes.

Constellation Challenge: Aquila the Eagle

Just north of Atlas is a star puzzle. When finished, it lights up in my favorite constellation, Aquila the Eagle. Above it looms an awesomely monumental depiction of an eagle brutalizing a chained Titan. I'd love a print of that for my dining hall.

Hey, Atlas . . . Hold This, Will You?

Atlas is strong as a Cretan ox team, but he chose to fight on the side of the Titans in their war against Olympos—such a classic meathead mistake. (Sure, he's a Titan too, but a smart operator would betray their family and go with the obvious winner.) When the big goons inevitably lost, I tossed most of them into the foulest pit of Tartaros . . . but not Atlas. No, I decided to make him hold up the sky on his shoulders for all eternity. Did I mention that Atlas's brother is Prometheus? God, I enjoy tormenting that family. I did toss Atlas a bone by letting him control storms and meteors and such.

This woman deserves a shrine. I feel bad about swallowing her, especially since she helped us get my dad, Kronos, to "unswallow" my siblings. Ironic, right? First, look for the statue of my dad just southwest of the Metis tower—yeah, the huge winged Titan jerk. If you can find the swaddled rock hidden nearby and put it in Kronos's hand . . . well, things warm up a bit, at least. Follow the now-lit torches upstairs to the navigation challenge. It leads you up to the Metis shrine and the gorgeous spear-wielding statue of my favorite fly-gal.

Constellation Challenge: The Great Bear

From the shrine, follow the path along the eastern cliffs overlooking the sea, lighting torches as you go. Eventually you reach another devilish constellation challenge. Once you complete this seven-star puzzle, you light up the bear constellation on the star panel. That's my gal Kallisto!

The next great tower is to the northwest, the Shrine of the Fates. But it isn't accessible until you complete a couple of myth challenges.

Constellation Challenge: Libra

First you solve a star puzzle that gives you the constellation Libra, depicting Athena's beloved scales of justice. As Prometheus has pointed out, Libra also symbolizes my own power to weigh mortal actions. Which reminds me of the creative swamps I had to slog through in order to design your wretched race.

Note: completing the Libra constellation challenge lights up the pathway for the nearby navigation challenge that leads up the mountain to the Shrine of the Fates. But keep an eye out for the fresco puzzle on the way up!

Fresco Challenge: Kronos Heaving

After you light up the torches around the puzzle stack for warmth, push the pieces together here to form the horrifying depiction of my drugged father puking up all of my siblings: Poseidon, Hades, Hera, Demeter, and Hestia. He also horked up boulders, some cattle, and the entire lyre section of the Athenian Philharmonic. What a mess that was.

What's the Buzz, Metis?

This clever river Nymph provided me with good counsel during the Titanomachy, and I made her my first wife. It was her brilliant idea to whip up the emetic my mother, Rhea, and I fed to Kronos so he'd regurgitate all my brothers and sisters that he'd swallowed. And she's a prophet to boot! But one night, Metis made the mistake of foretelling that one of my kids would overthrow me. As a result, when I later found out she was pregnant (with Athena, as it turns out), I goaded her into her favorite trick—turning into a fly—then I swallowed her. "Where's Metis?" everybody asked. I told them she was visiting her sister in Babylon. Today, years later, it's kind of insulting that nobody seems surprised she never came back. I wonder if she's still buzzing around inside me? That would be seriously weird.

Kallisto Is a Bear

Look, I really have a thing for minor nature deities. Something about them . . . the musk, maybe . . . really gets my juices flowing. This vivacious little sprite in the retinue of Artemis caught my eye. At first, Kallisto rebuffed my advances, saying she was fully devoted to that crazy Artemis Creed of Virginity. "I love only Artemis!" she cried. "Noted!" I said. Then I disguised myself as Artemis and had at her. Fun!

The tryst was wildly experimental, the way I like it, plus it produced a son, Arkas. (That kid eventually founded Arkadia. What can I say? Kinghood runs in my bloodline.) Of course, as always, my wife, Hera, found out about everything and turned Kallisto into a really big bear. To commemorate our saucy time together, I put her into the northern sky as a constellation—the Great Bear.

Mortal Combat 5.0

Look, I put a lot of work into you people. And I hate to say it, but I'm not feeling the love I deserve. It took me five tries to get to your current build . . . and frankly, now I'm thinking about a complete reboot. Here's the history: After we gods beat down on the Titans and I cast them into Tartaros, it felt safe to make some minions for our amusement. First, I fashioned a mortal race from gold. Their perfection was seriously boring—watching gold people is like drinking one of Persephone's sleep nectars. So, I wiped that slate clean and tried silver people. That was even worse—turns out, silver poisons the brain and makes you so stupid you slam into poles and blame socialism for everything.

Brass was next. Wow, big mistake. Brass is a very aggressive metal, apparently. Don't ever invite brass people to a dinner party. It was like one huge death match, day after day. So again, I swiped left, retried with a whole new source code, and came up with mortal heroes! Wow, these folks were almost godlike in their skills and wacky temperament. What a race! I loved them, but unfortunately, I jotted down the recipe on the back of a lottery ticket then accidentally tossed it out.

That led to the current build. That's you people. I used iron this time. From day one, your race has been characterized by warfare, lust, venality, selfishness, rash pursuit of power, and really poor hygiene. It's disgusting. I mean, who do you think you are? Gods? (If so, that's called hubris, and you can bet an actual god will inflict some misery until your pride is extinguished.)

Shrine of the Fates

The navigation challenge next to the Libra constellation puzzle runs you right up to the tower top where you find the Shrine of the Fates. I told you already about the Fates, AKA the Moirai, back during your tour of War's Den. These are my three daughters with Themis who totally control the "life thread" of every mortal—birth, length of life, and death.

Odysseus Challenge: Flaming Wheel of Ixion
Check out this crazy representation of the fate of poor stupid King Ixion. All you have to do is shoot a flaming arrow through about four zillion hoops, some held up by centaur statues—a nice ironic touch by Daidalos. No problem! When completed, the puzzle ignites a huge wheel nearby and sets it spinning too. I could stare at that thing for hours.

Fresco Challenge: The Banishment of Lykaon
Before you hustle to the spinning fire-wheel to start the navigation challenge, take the left path fork and follow it across the long stone bridge. Uphill to your right you find another fresco puzzle. I like this one because I look damn good in it. You have to unlock the puzzle first, but then move the pieces together to form a fresco of me, Zeus, driving off that ghoulish wolfman Lykaon.

Navigation Challenge: Wheel to Shrine
Now retrace your steps back to the big spinning replica of Ixion's fire-wheel. Step onto the trigger plate at the base then make the long, freezing sprint up to the Shrine of Themis atop the tower. Good luck. This one really sucks.

Ixion the Wheeler-Dealer
This guy's life is a tale of self-inflicted woe. During a dispute with his new wife's father,

Ixion pushed the old man into a pit of red-hot coals. Suddenly everyone was calling him "the Kin-Slayer" and he became an outcast, wandering like a beggar around Thessaly. I heard his supplications and took pity—hey, even kings make mistakes—by inviting him to hang out in my court on Mount Olympos.

But instead of thanks, what did I get? The guy tried to seduce my wife! Not cool. So first, I tricked Ixion into copulating with a cloud. (Check out the **Centaurs** *origin story below.) Then, I blasted him with a thunderbolt, my signature move. Finally, I had Hermes bind Ixion to a wagon wheel, set it on fire, and send it spinning for all eternity. Enjoy the never-ending carnival ride, Kin-Slayer!*

Hey, Kids, This Is Where Centaurs Come From!
This origin story is a real hoot. A mortal king named Ixion tried to seduce Hera, my wife—a self-destructive move if ever there was one—and of course I found out about it. But instead of just smiting the bastard, I decided it would be more fun to mess with his head. I shaped a cloud like Hera and breathed life into it. Totally fooled, Ixion hopped aboard her like a rutting goat! Me and my guys up here laughed so hard we broke ribs.

The funny thing is, Ixion actually managed to impregnate the cloud! Soon the cloud birthed a horribly deformed child named Centauros who was promptly banished from Ixion's kingdom. The miserable kid wandered around Thessaly until he found a pack of wild mares near Mount Pelion and started humping them left and right. The result of these unholy unions was a new race of

creatures: centaurs! Moral of the story: if you mess with Zeus's woman, you end up producing a line of monstrous grandkids who snort in glee as you spin around in flames, vomiting and burning, for eight bajillion years.

Lykaon's Lean Cuisine

This sick lunatic King Lykaon chopped up his own son Nyctimos and tried to serve him to me at a banquet. The reason: he doubted my omniscience and wanted to test it. Unfortunately for Lykaon, I figured it out after a few bites. (The human eyeball on the appetizer platter also gave it away.)

At first, I wanted to cast the demented ghoul deep into Tartaros, and I quickly blasted his 49 remaining sons into inedible bits of charcoal. But I thought it over, then decided to turn Lykaon into a foul, smelly werewolf instead.

I drove him off into the woods and yelled, Enjoy eating people, bitch! Later I heard his poor son Nyctimos was a good kid who certainly didn't have much going as a food item — man, he tasted terrible — so I let Gaia resurrect the boy. I hear he opened up a vegan restaurant in Corinth. I may drop in someday and convince him to serve wolf loin.

Shrine of Themis

Not really much to see up here. Thick shroud of falling snow, maybe a bear or two in the distance. Nice statue of Themis. At least I think it's Themis. Anyway, after you look around a bit, head on up to the real show.

Themis

As the first lady of law, fairness, and morality—and my second wife—Themis had a knack for doing the right thing, always. Sadly, that knack, combined with her Delphian skill of prophecy, made her a real ball buster to live with. Man, I was constantly in trouble for cheating with girls I hadn't even met yet. And the woman never yelled at me! She was like, "How do you feel about what you've done in the future, Zeus? Bad, I suspect?"

So beautiful, so balanced and pragmatic, with her calm voice and scales of justice. To this day, even Hera respectfully calls her "Lady Themis." (Hera brutally despises all my ex-consorts, but she's surprisingly cool about the ex-wives.) But the relationship was just too unnerving for me. When I finally got out of it, I had to go on a three-week bender with the Thessaly centaurs just to cleanse.

Okay, time to wrap up this book and our little tour. What better place to do so than right at the pinnacle of King's Peak—the high point of your little mortal world?

◇ ◇ ◇

Zeus's Throne: An Epilogue

That's right, this is it: Chryse's main attraction. The big chair, baby!

Sitting in it always makes me feel like some sort of superstar king of the gods, and then I remember, oh yeah, that's exactly who I am.

I've said it before and I'll say it again: it's really great to be me. Everybody thinks I'm pretty fantastic—my fellow gods and demigods and subgods and mortal heroes. My siblings, my kids (all fifty-four of them!). My lovers and ex-lovers. And all of you mortal sycophants. (Keep those gifts and offerings coming, folks!) Even my wife Hera . . . mostly.

Okay, maybe not Hera. Sometimes, I guess. Hey, she wouldn't be so catty and cruel to my lovers if she didn't secretly think I was worth it, right?

Two guys don't like me so much, though.

One is Typhon. Of course, who cares about him, he's a four-eyed monstrous dolt. Lately I've heard a lot of rumbling under the mountain I slammed on top of him. Gotta say, I love the thought of him down there in Tartaros, sulking, angry, stomping around and punching at the pillars where he's chained for all eternity.

The other is Prometheus. We have a complicated relationship, him and me. I find myself hanging out with him more, lately. The guy has an interesting take on things.

Maybe someday I'll call off Carl from his daily feasts. For a few days, maybe. Give them both a respite. If you had to eat liver every single day, you might get sick of it, I imagine. And the guy who you slash open to tear out his liver—I suppose he could use a break from routine too.

I'll have to think about a reprieve. His torment is just so much fun, though!

Well, I'm headed "downstairs" (ha ha) to visit my brother Hades. His oenology team is about to uncork a new Lethean vintage, and he wants me to sample it. It's nice to know I can take a break because Olympos is tight as a drum, and everything on Chryse is running smoothly too. The cowering fear I've instilled in the staff really keeps them hopping!

Yes, we've got a nice operation here on the Golden Isle. Be a shame if anything happened to it.

◇ ◇ ◇

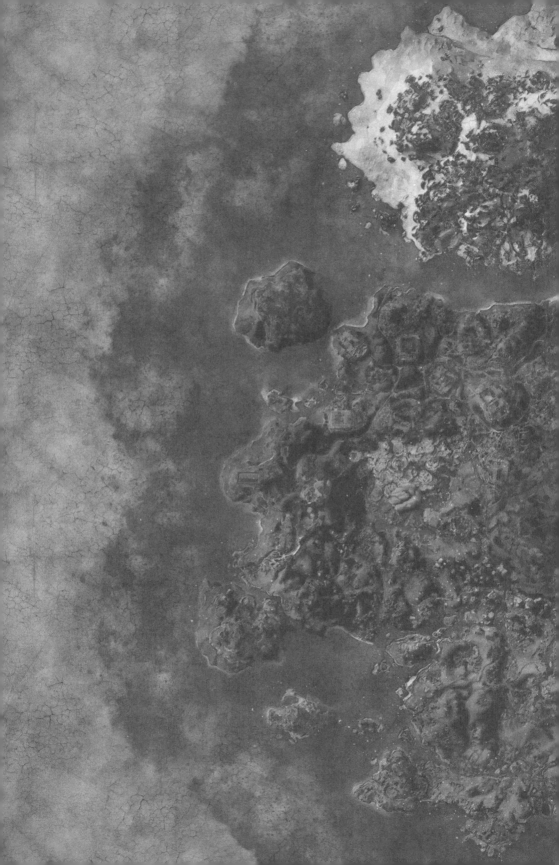